# BLUEPRINT

# Design & Technol
## Teacher's Resource
## Book
## Key Stage 1

**Tim Gadd**

**Stanley Thornes (Publishers) Ltd**

# Do you receive *BLUEPRINTS NEWS*?

Blueprints is an expanding series of practical teacher's ideas books and photocopiable resources for use in primary schools. Books are available for separate infant and junior age ranges for every core and foundation subject, as well as for an ever widening range of other primary teaching needs. These include **Blueprints Primary English** books and **Blueprints Resource Banks**. **Blueprints** are carefully structured around the demands of National Curriculum in England and Wales, but are used successfully by schools and teachers in Scotland, Northern Ireland and elsewhere.

**Blueprints** provide:
- *Total curriculum coverage*
- *Hundreds of practical ideas*
- *Books specifically for the age range you teach*
- *Flexible resources for the whole school or for individual teachers*
- *Excellent photocopiable sheets – ideal for assessment and children's work profiles*
- *Supreme value.*

Books may be bought by credit card over the telephone and information obtained on **(01242) 577944**. Alternatively, photocopy and return this **FREEPOST** form to receive **Blueprints News**, our regular update on all new and existing titles. You may also like to add the name of a friend who would be interested in being on the mailing list.

Please add my name to the **BLUEPRINTS NEWS** mailing list.

Mr/Mrs/Miss/Ms _____

Home address _____

_____ Postcode _____

School address _____

_____ Postcode _____

Please also send **BLUEPRINTS NEWS** to:

Mr/Mrs/Miss/Ms _____

Address _____

_____ Postcode _____

To: Marketing Services Dept., Stanley Thornes Ltd, FREEPOST (GR 782), Cheltenham, GL50 1BR

---

Text © Tim Gadd 1996
Original line illustrations by Mark Dunn, © ST(P) Ltd 1996

The right of Tim Gadd to be identified as the author of this work has been asserted by him in accordance with the Copyright, Designs and Patents Act 1988.

First published in 1996 by:
Stanley Thornes (Publishers) Ltd
Ellenborough House
Wellington Street
CHELTENHAM GL50 1YD
England

A catalogue record for this book is available from the British Library.
ISBN 0–7487–2388–9

Typeset by Tech Set Limited, Gateshead, Tyne & Wear
Printed and bound in Great Britain at The Bath Press, Avon

96 97 98 99 00 / 10 9 8 7 6 5 4 3 2 1

# CONTENTS

**Acknowledgements**

Stanley Cook: 'At Sea in the House', from *A Very First Poetry Book*, ed. John Foster, OUP © Stanley Cook; Gareth Owen: 'Cycling Down the Street to Meet my Friend John', from *Salford Road and Other Poems* by Gareth Owen, © Gareth Owen 1988, reproduced by permission of the author c/o Rogers, Coleridge & White Ltd., 20 Powis Mews, London W11 1JN; Mary Ann Hoberman: 'Tiger' from *Hello and Goodbye*, Little, Brown & Company, © Mary Ann Hoberman 1959 (renewed 1987).

Every effort has been made to trace all copyright holders but if any have been overlooked, the publishers will be pleased to make the necessary arrangements at the first opportunity.

# INTRODUCTION

The aim of these books is to provide teachers of Key Stage 1 Technology with ways of addressing the guidelines for the National Curriculum.

The suggested activities work on the premise that Design Technology is part of the normal classroom practice, although the key lessons in skill development allow for the fact that children's experience in technology might be limited.

*Blueprints Design & Technology KS1* addresses certain topic assignments, as well as design tasks that are intended to develop further technology skills, while not being topic specific.

The books refer to the KS1 programmes of study and offer opportunities to improve children's designing and making skills and thus develop their knowledge and understanding. The books aim to provide a realistically balanced approach to technology that allows children to work individually at their own level and also offer opportunities for group and cooperative work within the classroom.

The Teacher's Resource Book offers a wide range of ideas in technology that are supported by activities on Copymaster sheets in the separate Copymasters Book.

The Teacher's Resource Book is arranged in the following sections:

**Key Stage 1 Programmes of Study**
This section is broken down into the following areas:

Technology language
Key lessons: Design skills
Design tasks
Key lessons: Making skills
Topic assignments
Inspecting and disassembling products
Technology from poems
Technology from stories

**Techniques, Tools and Storage**
This section provides a resource of techniques in infant technology, focused on frameworks, structures, gears, cogs and pulleys, axles, wheels, joining materials and electrics. Advice is offered on the safe use of tools in the classroom, as well as storage ideas for resources.

**Resources Checklist**
This section provides a checklist of useful classroom resources, including consumable materials and construction kits that will support KS1 Technology.

# HOW TO USE THESE BOOKS

*Blueprints Design & Technology* is a resource that can be used in different ways to meet the needs of a particlar class of children. It can also be used to provide a framework for technology throughout a school.

The ideas in these books can be used as a starting point in one or more of the following ways.

**Key lessons in skill development**
There are a number of key lessons which are intended to establish skill development in the technology process.

**Design skills**
    Pattern
    Size and scale
    Shape

**Making skills**
    Using a pencil and a ruler
    Using scissors
    Folding
    Joining

**Knowledge and understanding**
    Technology language
    Key lessons in design and making skills
    Design tasks
    Topic assignments
    Evaluation

Copymasters 1–11 provide children with a discussion sheet and design planning sheets as well as record sheets to support their work in technology. There are 'visual checklists', a step chart and an evaluation sheet which can be applied to any or all tasks undertaken.

## Design tasks

These tasks provide opportunities for children to apply their design skills, established through the key lessons in design skills.

The design tasks are intended for children to undertake individually, or in small groups, focusing on the design and possible manufacture of the final product.

A space is provided on each task sheet to record the resources and equipment that could be used in each design.

## Focused practical tasks

These tasks provide an opportunity for children to experience the 'design and make' process. They are intended to encourage cooperative work and could be undertaken in pairs or in small groups.

They are not topic specific and provide opportunities for children to operate fairly independently of the teacher, only seeking advice and help where necessary. These tasks can be approached when the children have established basic design and making skills, addressed in the key lessons.

## Topic assignments

Teachers may want to use these suggestions as a basis for classroom technology. The following topics are included:

Weather
Movement in air
Buildings and structures
Travel and movement
Electricity
Movement in water
Sound
Leverage
Gravity
Manipulation of materials

Teachers can refer to the Topic Planners on pages viii/ix. Evaluation sheets for these topics are provided throughout the book in the relevant sections.

## Inspecting and disassembling products

As part of the *National Curriculum Programme of Study*, children are expected to undertake activities in which they investigate and disassemble simple products.

*Blueprints Design & Technology* advises teachers to obtain the following five products:

Stapler
Hole punch
Cereal box
Picture frame
Torch

Copymasters with detailed drawings of these items are available for completion by the children.

## Technology from poems and stories

Poems and stories are an essential part of the infant curriculum and can provide many exciting and stimulating opportunities for technology. There are several poems and stories presented for teachers to use in technology work, which offer an opportunity to display the children's work in school, with the poem or story as the centrepiece of that display.

# STARTING FROM PROGRAMMES OF STUDY ▶

The National Curriculum requires that pupils should be given:

- assignments in which they design and make:
- focused practical tasks;
- investigations and disassembling activities.

*Blueprints Design & Technology* offers:

- topic assignments;
- design tasks;
- inspecting and disassembling activities.

---

Pupils should be given opportunities to:

- work with range of materials and components;
- investigate the working characteristics of materials which happen to suit different purposes;
- apply skills and knowledge to other subject areas.

- tasks and assignments that involve working with many materials;
- work with clay, paper, wood, plastic and electricity;
- opportunities to involve cross curricula links through topic assignments.

---

Pupils should be taught to:

- draw on their own experience to help generate ideas;
- clarify their ideas through discussion;
- develop their ideas through shaping, assembling and rearranging materials and components;
- develop and communicate their design ideas by making freehand drawings, and by modelling their ideas in other ways;
- make suggestions about how to proceed;
- consider their design ideas as these develop, and identify strengths and weaknesses.

opportunities to:

- discuss;
- plan;
- make drawings;
- design;
- evaluate.

---

Pupils should be taught to:

- select materials, tools and techniques;
- measure, mark out, cut and shape a range of materials;
- assemble, join and combine materials and components;
- apply simple finishing techniques;
- make suggestions about how to proceed;
- evaluate their products as these are developed, identifying strengths and weaknesses.

opportunities to:

- consider design;
- consider resources;
- select materials and tools;
- assemble, join and combine materials;
- evaluate, modify, improve products.

---

Pupils should be taught:

- to use simple mechanisms, including wheels, axles and joints;
- to make structures more stable and withstand greater loads;
- to investigate and disassemble simple products;
- to relate the ways things work to their intended purpose;
- that the quality of a product depends on how well it is made and how well it suits its purpose;
- simple knowledge and understanding of health and safety;
- to use appropriate vocabulary for naming and describing the equipment, materials and components they use.

opportunities to:

- design and make simple mechanisms;
- make stable structures to withstand loads;
- inspect and disassemble easily available product and therefore consider the quality and suitability to the purpose of that product;
- learn good, safe working habits when using tools, equipment and materials;
- learn and use appropriate technology vocabulary.

# TOPIC PLANNERS

These planners will enable you to locate teacher's notes and Copymasters related to specific tasks and assignments.

| TOPIC | TEACHER'S NOTES | PAGE | COPYMASTER |
|---|---|---|---|
| Weather | Thunder maker | 24 | |
| | Weather chart | 25 | 71 |
| | Rain gauge | 26 | |
| Movement in air | Helicopter | 27 | 73, 74 |
| | Parachute | 28 | 75 |
| | Hovercraft | 29 | |
| | Aeroplane wing | 30 | |
| Buildings and structures | Cross sections | 31 | |
| | Pillars | 32 | 78, 79 |
| | Bridging a gap | 33 | 80, 81 |
| | Houses: 1 ('box' model) | 34 | |
| | Houses: 2 (framework) | 35 | |
| | Furniture | 36 | |
| Travel and movement | Tipper truck | 39 | |
| | Simple powered vehicles | 40 | |
| | Easy wheeled vehicle | 41 | 83–87 |
| | Simple vehicle with axle and wheels | 42 | |
| | Hydraulics | 43 | |
| Electricity | Simple circuit and switch | 44 | 89 |
| | Circuit board game | 45 | 90 |
| | Paint spinner | 46 | |
| Movement in water | Ships and boats | 47 | 92 |
| | Diving bell | 48 | |
| Sound | Percussion instruments | 49 | 94 |
| Leverage | Creature with moving ears | 51 | |
| | Gate barrier | 52 | |
| Gravity | Balancing clown | 53 | 95 |
| | Balancing bird | 54 | 96 |
| Manipulation of materials | Clay work: 1 | 55 | |
| | Claywork: 2 | 56 | |
| | Pop-up card | 57 | |
| | Decorated card box | 58 | |

These planners will enable you to locate teacher's notes and Copymasters related to specific tasks and assignments.

| TOPIC | TEACHER'S NOTES | PAGE | COPYMASTER |
|---|---|---|---|
| Inspecting and disassembling products | Stapler | 59 | 97 |
| | Cereal box | 59 | 98 |
| | Hole punch | 59 | 99 |
| | Picture frame | 59 | 100 |
| | Torch | 59 | 101 |
| | | | |
| Technology from poems | The Firemen | 61 | 102 |
| | Mummy, Oh Mummy | 62 | 103 |
| | Where? | 63 | |
| | Christmas Secrets | 65 | |
| | Cycling Down the Street to | | |
| | Meet My Friend John | 66 | 104 |
| | Clock | 67 | 105 |
| | Jamaica Market | 68 | |
| | At Sea in the House | 69 | |
| | The Bird's Nest | 70 | |
| | Tiger | 71 | |
| | | | |
| Technology from stories | The Trouble with Dad | 72 | |
| | Pinny's Party | 74 | 106 |
| | Gran Builds a House | 75 | |
| | My Presents | 77 | |
| | What's the Time Mr Wolf | 78 | 107, 108 |

# SKILLS DEVELOPMENT CHART

| KEY LESSONS | TEACHER'S NOTES | PAGE | COPYMASTER |
|---|---|---|---|
| Design skills | Pattern | 10 | 12, 13, 14 |
| | Size and scale | 10 | 6 |
| | Shape | 10 | 5 |
| | Badges | | 15 |
| | Bookmark | | 16 |
| | Plans | | 17–19 |
| Design tasks | Puppet theatre | 12 | 29 |
| | Design a mask | 13 | 20 |
| | Design a party hat | 14 | 21 |
| | Design a badge | 15 | 15, 25 |
| | Menu shapes | 16 | 27, 51 |
| | Storyboard sheet | 17 | 26 |
| | Playground markings | 18 | 23 |
| | Book cover | | 22 |
| | Doll's costume | | 24 |
| | Playground seat | | 28 |
| | Toy that rocks | | 30 |
| | Bedroom plan | | 31 |
| | Crane | | 46 |
| | Move a heavy block | | 47 |
| | Mobile | | 48 |
| | Greetings card | | 49 |
| | Lunch box | | 50 |
| | Hand puppet | | 52 |
| | Egg holder | | 53 |
| | Finger puppet | | 54 |
| | Pram or trolley | | 55 |
| | Wind vane | | 56 |
| | Christmas tree decoration | | 57 |
| | Table decoration | | 58 |
| | Calendar | | 59 |
| | Model binoculars | | 60 |
| | Eye chart | | 61 |
| | Model stethoscope | | 62 |
| | Jigsaw puzzle | | 63 |
| | Magnet game | | 64 |
| | Poster | | 65 |
| | Model creature | | 66 |
| | Model person | | 67 |
| | Model town | | 68 |
| | School flag | | 69 |
| | Clay fossil | | 70 |

| KEY LESSONS | TEACHER'S NOTES | PAGE | COPYMASTER |
|---|---|---|---|
| Making skills | Using a pencil and a ruler | 20 | 32–35 |
| | Using scissors | 20 | 36–38 |
| | Folding: simple folding book (No. 1) | 21 | 40 |
| | Folding: simple folding book (No. 2) | 22 | 41 |
| | Joining | 22 | 42–45 |

| RECORD/EVALUATION SHEETS | PAGE | COPYMASTER |
|---|---|---|
| Record sheets | 5, 95, 96 | 7–10 |
| Evaluation sheets | | 11, 72, 76, 82, 88, 91, 93 |

**Design Skills**

| ENGLAND NATIONAL CURRICULUM AND WALES | SCOTLAND NATIONAL GUIDELINES | BLUEPRINTS TECHNOLOGY |
|---|---|---|
| Draw on own experiences to help generate ideas.<br><br>Discussion of ideas: assembling, shaping and re-arranging materials.<br><br>Communicate ideas: drawings, notes and prototype models.<br><br>Suggest ways to proceed and discuss these suggestions.<br><br>Evaluate the design: amend and modify. | Consider different ways of approaching a task: step by step, trying something different.<br><br>Discuss with group or teacher.<br><br>Plan simple steps for designing and solving design problems.<br><br>Propose headings to help group or organise information.<br><br>Propose simple methods of presenting design ideas: drawings, notes and simple models.<br><br>Record plans by drawing pictures, lists or captions. | Group discussion sheet (brainstorm).<br><br>Design sheets:<br>    squared<br>    plain.<br><br>Step chart 1–16 steps.<br><br>ID sheet Tools/equipment.<br><br>Record sheet: Tools/equipment.<br><br>Evaluation sheets to help amend and modify a product.<br><br>Design tasks:<br>    pattern<br>    size and scale<br>    shape.<br><br>Twelve 'open ended' design tasks. |

**Making Skills**

| ENGLAND NATIONAL CURRICULUM AND WALES | SCOTLAND NATIONAL GUIDELINES | BLUEPRINTS TECHNOLOGY |
|---|---|---|
| Select materials, tools and techniques.<br><br>Measure, mark out, cut and shape a range of materials.<br><br>Assemble, join, combine materials and components.<br><br>Apply finishing technique (painting).<br><br>Suggest procedures.<br><br>Evaluate, modify and discuss the product. | Make efficient and safe use of tools and equipment.<br><br>Follow simple written or pictorial instructions.<br><br>Carry out a simple task according to a plan.<br><br>Carry out a design task to meet certain criteria.<br><br>Present work and give a brief oral report.<br><br>Cooperate with others to create a display of work. | Tools/equipment selection sheet.<br><br>Exercises in making skills:<br>    using a ruler and a pencil<br>    using scissors<br>    folding<br>    joining.<br><br>Design sheets.<br><br>Evaluation sheets.<br><br>Group discussion recording sheet for ideas/procedures.<br><br>Tasks and assignment sheets. |

Children are asked to shade in the boxes to indicate the tools/materials to be used. To reinforce technology vocabulary, children can list the names of their chosen tool/materials in the spaces provided.

**What I will use**

| | |
|---|---|
| | |
| | |
| | |

# TECHNOLOGY LANGUAGE

This sheet could be enlarged and used as a wall chart.

**Shade in the boxes to show what you will use**

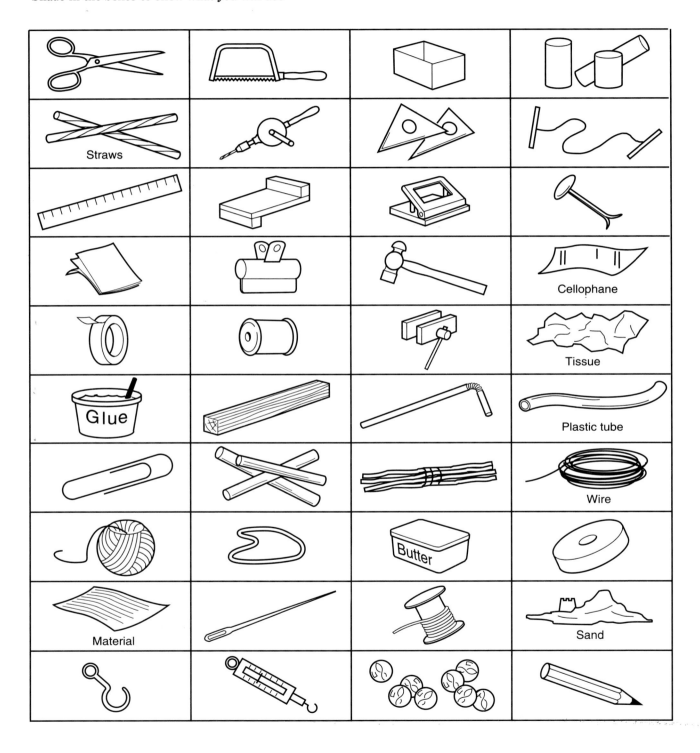

Straws

Cellophane

Tissue

Glue

Plastic tube

Wire

Butter

Material

Sand

**Design and make**

Children should be encouraged to

- Design
- Plan
- Make
- Evaluate

These processes form a vital part of technology as it is the transfer from 2D to 3D reality. The design and make process develops skills and concepts such as estimation, awareness of shape, scale and size, and drawing and measuring, all of which are fundamental to a successful outcome.

Children can develop and improve language skills through discussion of ideas, learn relevant appropriate technology vocabulary and clarity in presenting ideas to others. The evaluation of a project presents the opportunity for positive and constructive feedback. Children's experiences in technology will hopefully develop their confidence to examine critically their own designs without the fear and disappointment of being 'wrong'.

*Implications for the teacher*

Resources will need to be plentiful and it may help to consider the three As:

- Availability of
- Accessibility of ⎱ Resources
- Appropriateness of ⎰

Work space is vital as it will allow for movement, as well as providing room for drawings, equipment and the safe use of tools.

When operating in a group, an exchange of ideas is important and writing down or drawing initial ideas gives a basis from which to start. Delegation of tasks, such as scribe or artist, will help a group to operate and cooperate more efficiently and effectively.

Consider *where* plans, designs and drawings can be placed while the children are working on their projects, as they will need to refer to drawings and plans during this process. (Perhaps clipped to an easel?)

Children may raise a lot of issues and questions and will need to consider points such as:

- What will my model look like?
- What size will it be?
- Will it move, turn, or balance?
- How will it be fastened together?
- Which materials will be needed?
- Will it do what I want it to?

Plain and squared design sheets are provided on Copymasters 2 and 3, which could be enlarged if necessary. A child's plan and design sheets can be kept as part of their records and as a source of evidence of the technology work they have done.

*Blueprints Design & Technology* provides a suggestion as to how records could be kept in the form of record/progress sheets when monitoring children's development. These can be found on pages 95 and 96.

7

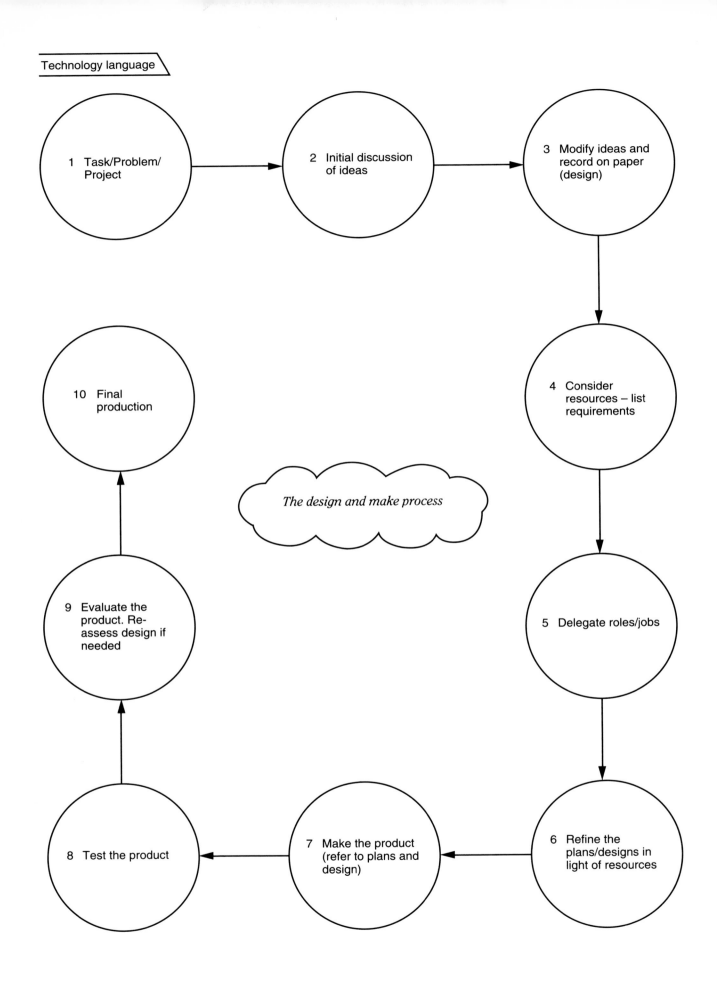

1   Task/Problem/Project

2   Initial discussion of ideas

3   Modify ideas and record on paper (design)

4   Consider resources – list requirements

*The design and make process*

10   Final production

9   Evaluate the product. Re-assess design if needed

5   Delegate roles/jobs

8   Test the product

7   Make the product (refer to plans and design)

6   Refine the plans/designs in light of resources

# KEY LESSONS:
# DESIGN SKILLS

# PATTERN ▶

## Aims
● To increase awareness of pattern in everyday life (e.g. wallpaper, fabrics, clothing).
● To help to stimulate ideas for children's own designs in pattern.

## Equipment/tools
Copymasters 12–14, patterns, pencil, colouring equipment (e.g. pencils, paint, crayons)

## Notes
● These tasks give the opportunity for children to complete existing patterns and also produce some of their own in a similar style.
● Looking at wallpaper books, disc and CD covers, magazine advertisements, etc. will reveal many patterns in their design. If may be helpful to have a supply available if possible.
● The Bookmark is entirely personal and children could produce pictures rather than pattern if they so wished.
● The badge-making task is an opportunity to produce a pattern or picture linked to a specific idea. It may be symbolic, patterned, a logo, or a picture as appropriate. Some badge shapes are provided on the Copymaster as well as the opportunity for children to decide their own pattern on the design to decorate this.

The children should not necessarily be expected to complete *all* the blanks as they are intended to act only as a starting point for ideas.

# SIZE AND SCALE ▶

## Aims
● To consider the size and scale of the object or model to be made.
● To encourage children to make their model an appropriate, sensible size to handle, build and modify.
● To increase the understanding that the finished product is determined in part by available resources.

## Equipment/tools
Copymasters 4–6

## Notes
● Children need to consider the scale of the model before starting any design drawings.
● Children need to consider the size of the model they are planning.
● Task delegation within a working group needs to be organised.
● Full consideration needs to be given to the resources that are available, and how they will influence the outcome (e.g. shape of boxes, lengths of wood).

Copymaster 6 addresses this issue by asking the children to make simple comparisons of size with everyday objects.

# SHAPE ▶

## Aims
● To encourage consideration of the shape of the product to be made.
● To increase awareness that the outcome will be determined in part by available resources.

## Equipment/tools
Copymaster 5

## Notes
● Teachers will need to consider the 'three As'
(availability, accessibility, appropriateness) when gathering resource materials for use in technology.
● The wider the range of materials the better, and if possible stored in such a way as to be easily accessible to children.
● The availability of resources may be influenced by funding, or children's response to bringing things from home.

# DESIGN TASKS

These tasks provide opportunities for children to apply the skills established through the key lessons in design skills.

The design tasks are intended for children to undertake individually or in small groups, focusing on the design and possible manufacture of the final product. A space is provided on each task sheet to record the resources and equipment that could be used in each design.

# PUPPET THEATRE – QUICK IDEAS!

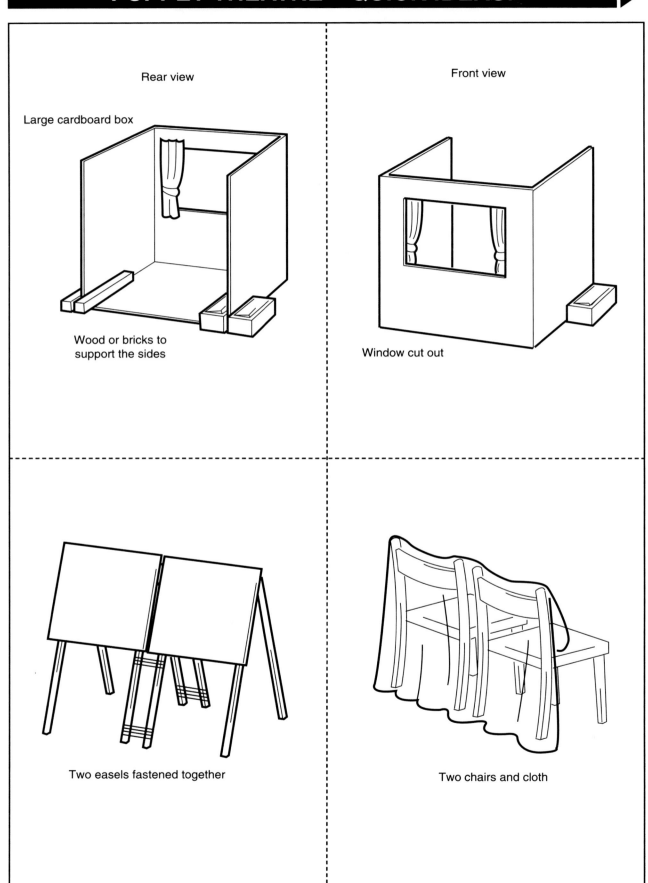

Rear view

Large cardboard box

Wood or bricks to
support the sides

Front view

Window cut out

Two easels fastened together

Two chairs and cloth

# DESIGN A MASK

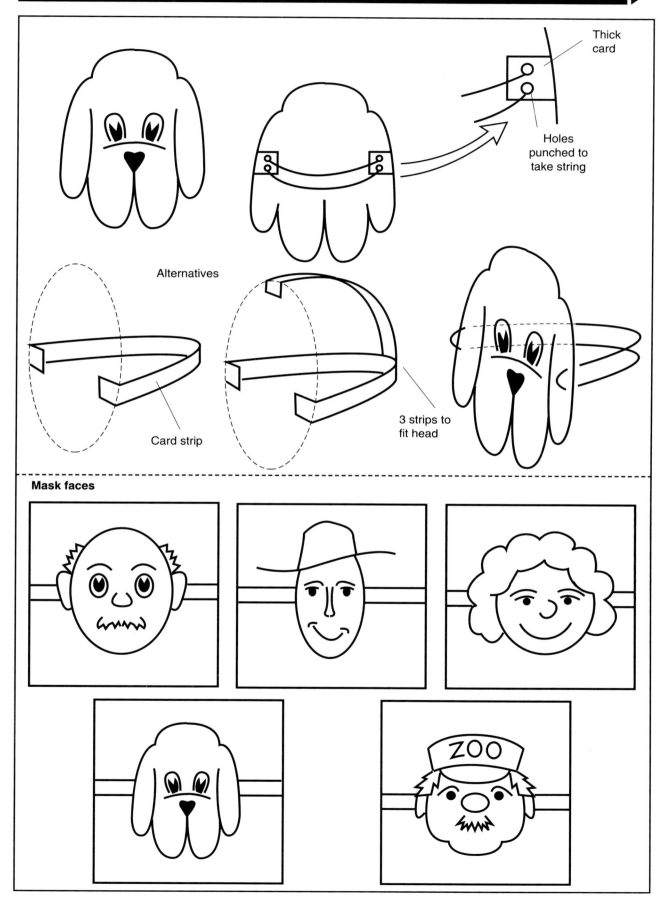

Thick card

Holes punched to take string

Alternatives

Card strip

3 strips to fit head

**Mask faces**

ZOO

# DESIGN A PARTY HAT

Top hat type

Glue tabs

Simple crown

Spiky hair

Card strip over the head

Stick shapes round the rim

14

# DESIGN A BADGE

Cat lover

Dog lover

Birdwatcher

Bookworm

Helper's badge

Artist

Athlete's badge

# MENU SHAPES

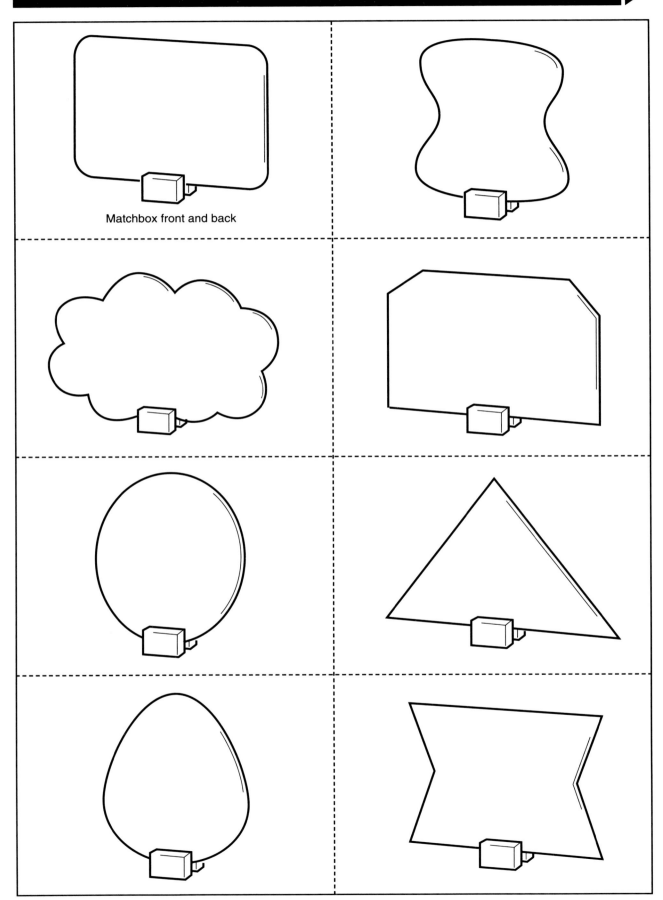

Matchbox front and back

# STORYBOARD SHEET

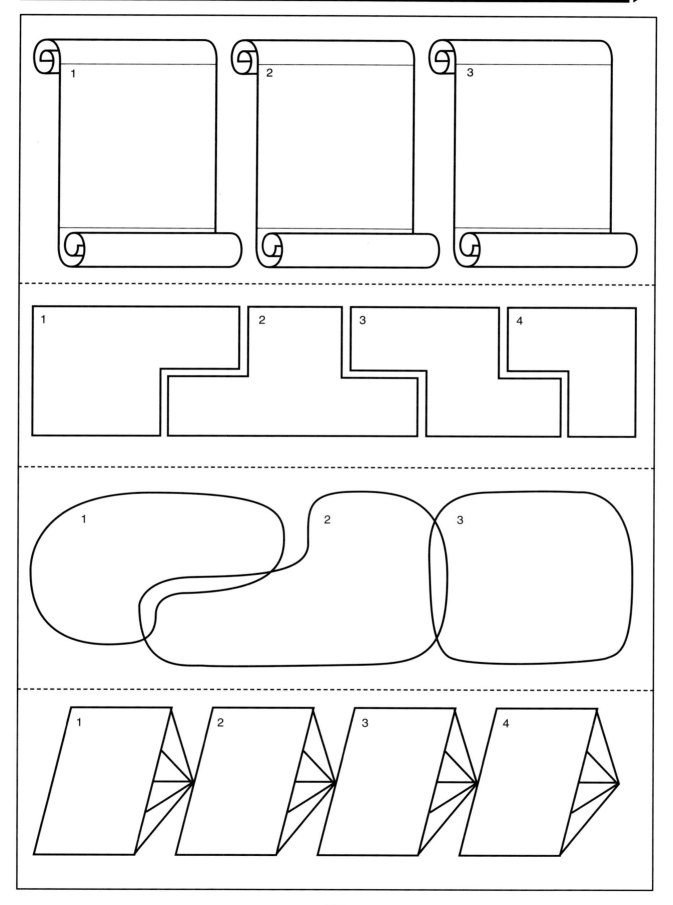

# PLAYGROUND MARKINGS

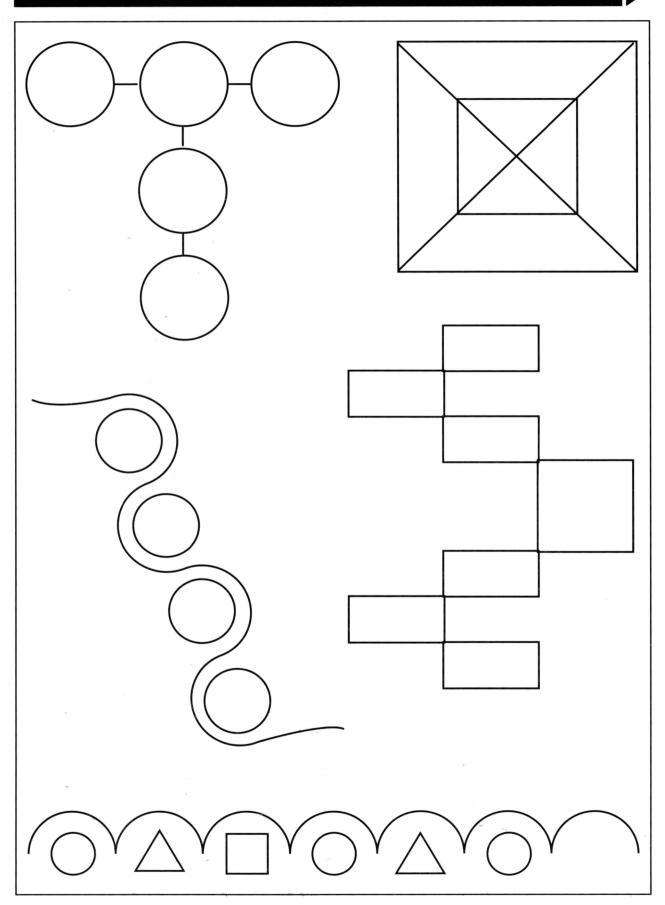

# KEY LESSONS:
# MAKING SKILLS

# USING A RULER AND A PENCIL

### Aims
● To establish the importance of using a ruler and pencil carefully and accurately to assist technology work.

### Equipment/tools
Copymasters 32–5, pencil, ruler

### Notes
● The use of a ruler and pencil is obviously a basic requirement in many curriculum areas, including technology.
● The aim of these exercises is to provide opportunities for the teacher to establish and develop good practice in using ruler and pencil.

### Points to stress
● The point of the pencil/pen must always be visible during use (rule along the top edge).
● The fingers should not interfere with the ruling of a line (keep them clear of the top edge of the ruler).
● Spread the fingers wide when holding down the ruler to avoid the ruler slipping.

When *measuring* and ruling lines, the start and finish of the drawn line should be accurately plotted. (See page 90. Copymaster 34 also addresses this point.) Precision will become very important in later stages, during technology assignments, when making things 'fit' or 'work' depends on the accuracy of measurement and cutting.

# USING SCISSORS

### Aims
● To provide support material for teachers when they are establishing and developing 'scissor skills'.

### Equipment/tools
Copymasters 36–8, scissors, pencils, crayons

### Notes
● Using scissors can safely be regarded as a basic skill in all curriculum areas and will no doubt be planned for in Art and Craft lessons, etc. The *accurate* use of scissors in technology is an essential, and the Copymasters try to provide opportunities to develop precision cutting.
● Cutting in a 'zig-zag' fashion can be done very successfully if the cuts are made separately from the outside edge every time.

● Copymaster 37 gives children the chance to become familiar with technology symbols/drawings used in this book. A similar exercise is used in the design and record-keeping section, when children are asked to record which equipment/tools they have used on a particular project. (Copymasters 7 and 8.)
● Copymaster 38 provides an opportunity to cut out and match numbers and shapes. (Cut from the top grid and glue in the correct place on the lower grid.)

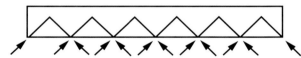

*Direction of cuts*

# FOLDING: SIMPLE FOLDING BOOK (NO. 1)

### Aims
● To emphasise the need for accuracy and care when folding paper.
● To develop manipulative skills.
● To improve the ability to follow a visual guide.

### Equipment/tools
Copymasters 39–41, A4 paper

### Notes
● Children will benefit from a key lesson in creating a 'sharp' fold (between finger and thumb) by folding on a line. This is a fairly simple task but one that depends on accuracy.

**Step 1** Fold along the centre line (AB)
**Step 2** Fold on the vertical lines in a concertina fashion
**Step 3** Children have made a simple folding book
**Step 4** Write and illustrate the book!

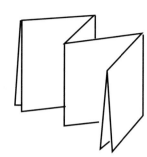

**Copymaster 40 looks like this**

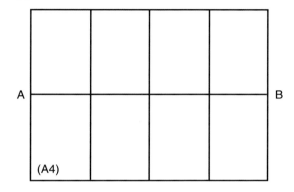

# FOLDING: SIMPLE FOLDING BOOK (NO. 2)

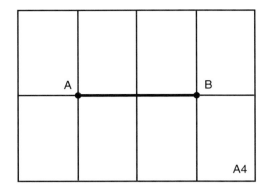

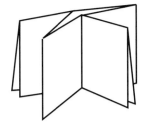

*Wrap the sides round to create this folding book*

**Aims**
● To emphasise the need for accuracy and care when folding.
● To develop manipulative skills.
● To develop the ability to follow a visual guide.

**Equipment/tools**
Copymaster 41, scissors

**Notes**
● Children will have the Copymaster ready ruled to fold and cut.
● Help and advice will be needed when cutting, indeed, some teachers may prefer to do this themselves.
● Small group or class activity.

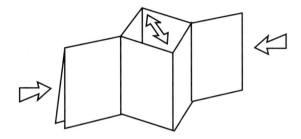

# JOINING

**Aims**
● To understand how materials can be joined together successfully, using available resources in the classroom.
● To experience the handling of different materials.
● To consider the suitability of various materials for future tasks and projects.

**Equipment/tools**
Copymasters 42–5, paper, wood, plastic, stone, straws, rubber, paper fasteners, staples, string, glue

**Notes**
● Children will discover that certain materials are easy to join together and others are most difficult.
● Resources will need to be prepared in advance to avoid waste.
● The joining together of materials is clearly fundamental in design technology, and experience and knowledge of 'joining' could enhance further assignments.

# TOPIC
# ASSIGNMENTS

# MAKING YOUR OWN THUNDER

### Aims
● To make children aware that when air is heated and moved by lightning it causes thunder.
● To understand that thunder is the sound made by lightning.

### Note
● The paper square should be glued to the card along *two* edges.

### Equipment/tools
Paper 20 cm × 20 cm – cut diagonally, card 20 cm × 20 cm, scissors, ruler, glue

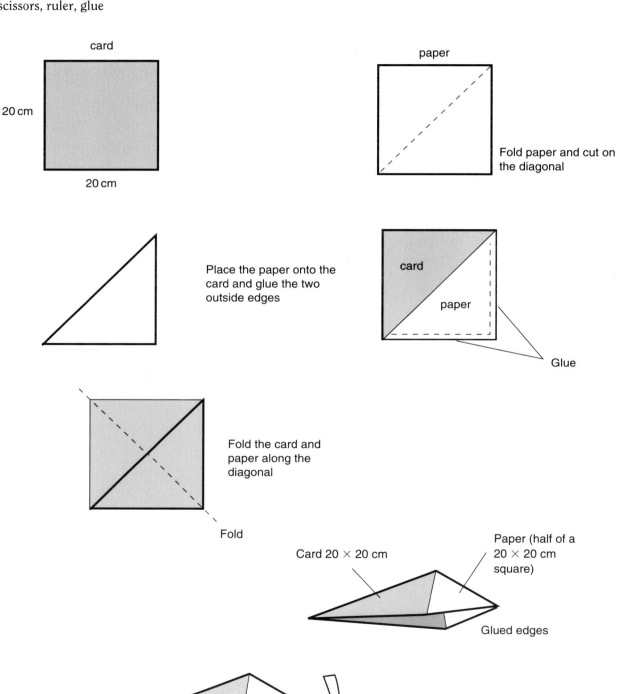

card

20 cm

20 cm

paper

Fold paper and cut on the diagonal

Place the paper onto the card and glue the two outside edges

card

paper

Glue

Fold the card and paper along the diagonal

Fold

Card 20 × 20 cm

Paper (half of a 20 × 20 cm square)

Glued edges

Shake quickly downwards to produce a 'thunder clap'

24

# WEATHER CHART

## Aims
● To help children to understand the use of symbols when displaying information.

## Equipment/tools
Copymaster 71, paper 30 × 30 cm, card 30 × 50 cm, scissors, glue, ruler, paper fasteners, pencil, crayons/paint

## Some suggested symbols

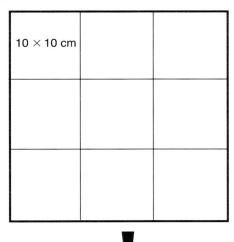

## Notes on various cloud types
Stratus: low, grey, often with showers
Nimbus: low, thick, usually dark, rain
Cirrus: high, sunny days, very cold nights
Cumulus: central height, 'cotton wool', usually with fine weather

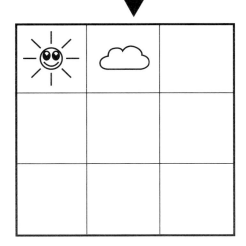

## Notes
● The paper needs to be ruled into 10 × 10 cm squares.
● Selected symbols can be drawn in these squares, before cutting them out (each one could be mounted on a coloured background if so wished).
● The card 30 × 50 cm is the actual board to which the symbols or picture can be secured with paper fasteners.

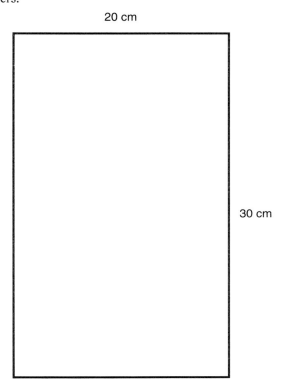

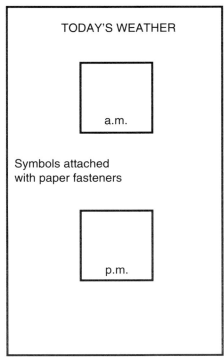

25

# RAIN GAUGE

### Aims

● To increase awareness of keeping weather records and their usefulness.
● To understand how a rain gauge works.
● To appreciate accuracy in keeping records.
● To collect, read and interpret data.

### Equipment/tools

Plastic bottle, scissors

### Notes

● The activity is fairly simple, involving cutting, pouring water, measuring and calibrating, which is the most difficult part.
● It is important to take regular readings from the rain gauge.

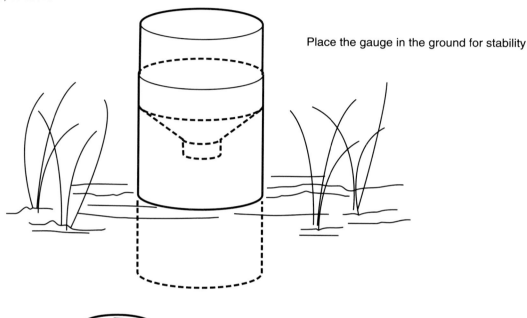

Place the gauge in the ground for stability

The rainfall can be measured fairly accurately in a test tube (or similar)

If water is poured into the plastic bottle to 5 mm depth – then transferred to the test tube which can then be graduated into mm divisions – the rainfall is easy to read in a test tube

Results of rainfall can be measured daily, weekly or to suit your needs and the results can be graphed.

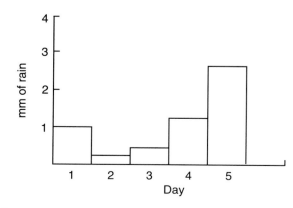

# HELICOPTER

### Aims
● To help children understand that an upward force, called *air resistance*, is exerted when objects fall through the air.

● To understand that the size and surface area of a falling object is important because it affects the speed of the downward movement of the object.

### Equipment/tools
Copymaster 73–4, paper, scissors, paper clip, paper fastener, Blu-tack

### Note
● The 'helicopters' spin as they fall because of air resistance beneath the wings. Children can experiment with different shaped wings and note the effect.

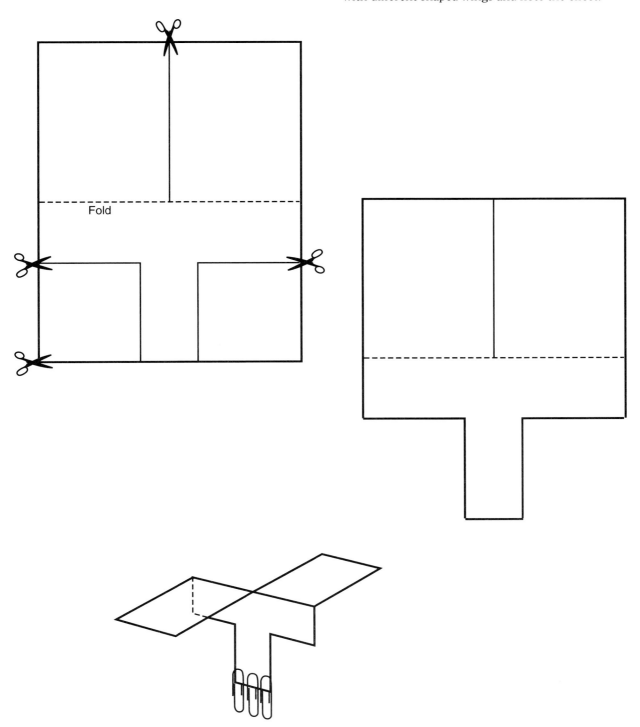

Attach weight
(paper clip, fastener, Blu-tack)

# PARACHUTE

## Aims

● To help children to understand resistance.

## Equipment/tools

Copymaster 75, pencil, hole punch, string, paper, material for parachute (plastic bag, cloth, paper, card) Blu-tack

## Cross curricula links

Science, Maths, Art, Language.

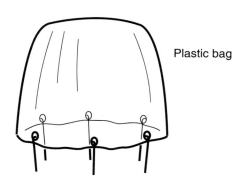

Plastic bag

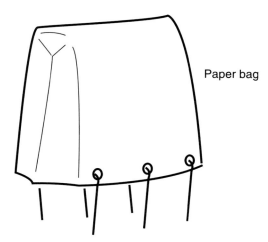

Paper bag

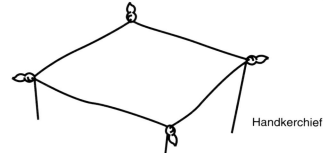

Handkerchief

The basket can be made from a 'net'

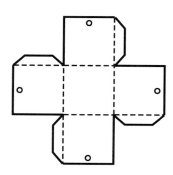

It is possible that the descent of the parachute will not be straight and smooth! Once this has been observed get the children to cut a small hole in the centre of the parachute and see if it changes anything.

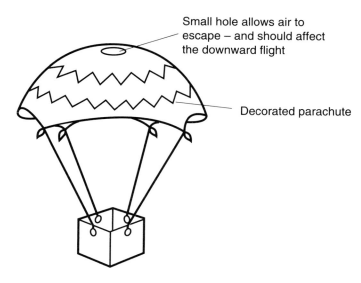

Small hole allows air to escape – and should affect the downward flight

Decorated parachute

28

# BRIDGING A GAP

## Aims

● To present a problem solving situation to the children (one that has many solutions!)
● To increase awareness of the span and strength needed to build a practical bridge.
● To test the bridge for stability and strength.

## Equipment/tools

Copymasters 80–1, selection of wood pieces, card, glue, scissors, paper, weights, string, ruler, pencil, construction kit (Lego®?)

## Notes

● This problem can be tackled by a group of children.
● It may be helpful for the group to delegate particular tasks to each member (recording, cutting, testing).
● Many solutions are possible – hence the need to *plan and design* before building the final version (design sheet!) (The use of cross-sections covered on page 31 may be helpful).
● The gap should not be too wide as to be impractical – (suggest 30 cm maximum).

### Some types of bridges

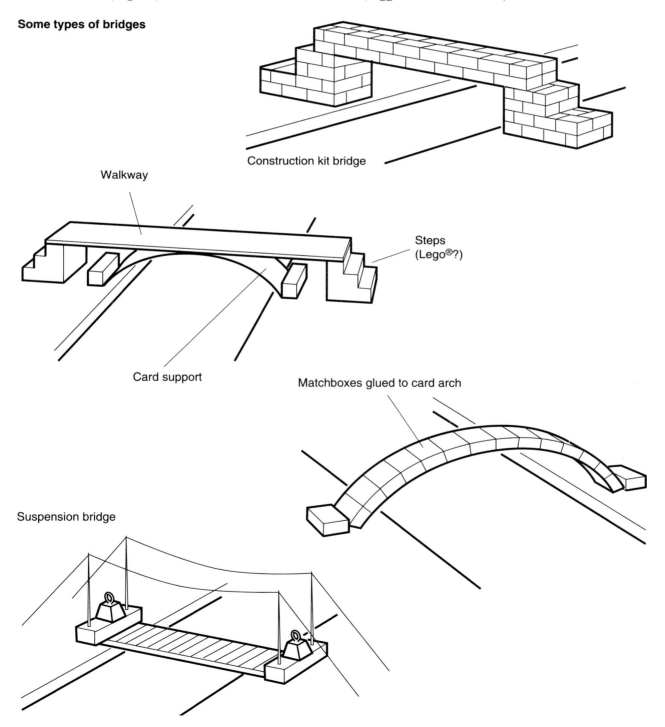

Construction kit bridge

Walkway

Steps
(Lego®?)

Card support

Matchboxes glued to card arch

Suspension bridge

33

# HOUSES: 1

## Aims

● To help children to build a simple 'box' house.
● To develop manipulative skills.
● To increase awareness of designing a project/assignment.

## Equipment/tools

Boxes of various sizes, glue, scissors, ruler, sellotape, paper fasteners, cellophane

## Notes

● Infant children will benefit from being able to create a model house quickly and simply.
● Looking at houses around the school area will reveal a variety of structures (old and new), and could provide a starting point for study.
● Houses in History (Tudor, Saxon etc.) make interesting comparisons with present-day buildings. Some help may be required if children find difficulty in cutting cardboard boxes with scissors.

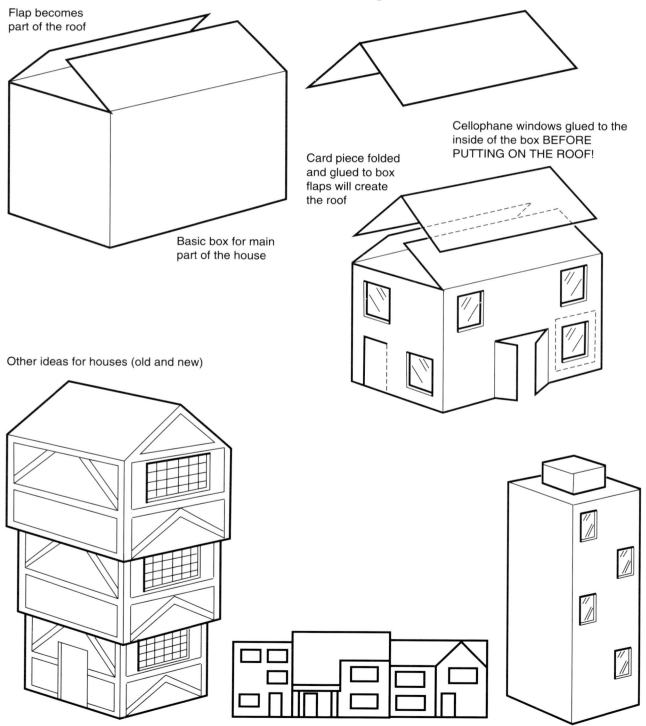

Flap becomes part of the roof

Basic box for main part of the house

Card piece folded and glued to box flaps will create the roof

Cellophane windows glued to the inside of the box BEFORE PUTTING ON THE ROOF!

Other ideas for houses (old and new)

# HOUSES: 2

## Aims
● To help children to understand and produce a simple framework structure.
● To develop manipulative skills using basic technology tools and skills.

## Equipment/tools
Square section wood 8 mm, card triangles, glue, scissors, card for house walls and roof, tubes or small boxes for chimneys

## Notes
● A simple house structure ('framework' type) gives an opportunity to apply the 'wood and card triangle' technique to a building project.
● The 'skills' section of the book will be helpful at this point.

## Cross curricula links
Geography, Science, History, Art

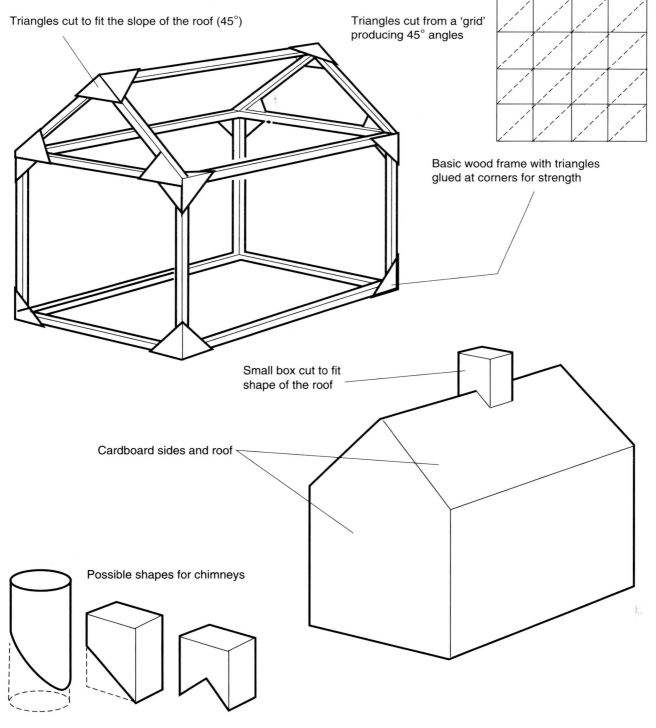

Triangles cut to fit the slope of the roof (45°)

Triangles cut from a 'grid' producing 45° angles

Basic wood frame with triangles glued at corners for strength

Small box cut to fit shape of the roof

Cardboard sides and roof

Possible shapes for chimneys

# FURNITURE

## Aims
● To develop the manipulative skills needed in technology.
● To develop design skills.
● To increase awareness of how objects are made to be stable and strong enough for use.

## Equipment/tools
Range of wood pieces (8 mm square), dowelling, glue, saw, bench hook, ruler, pencil, card, paper, scissors

## Notes
● By asking children to look at the classroom furniture it is possible to make them aware of legs/castors/feet, doors, drawers, moving parts (opening and closing), ladders.
● Practice in using tools/equipment and observation of safety measures is essential before using saws and bench hooks. (See 'Techniques, tools and storage', pp. 90–91)
● The availability and appropriateness of the resources available will help determine the choice of furniture to be made.

### Cot/bed

Turn the box over to create a 'flat top' if preferred

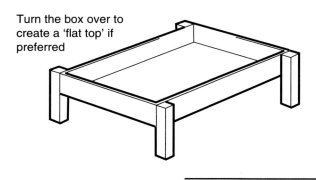

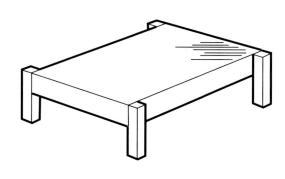

### Table

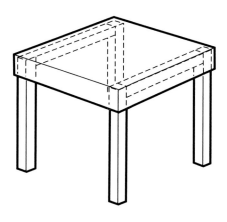

Card

Glue top to base

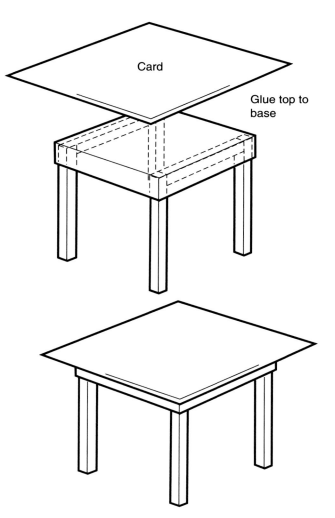

Supporting piece

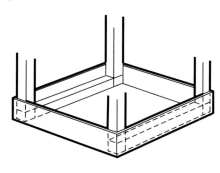

36

# HYDRAULICS (SYRINGES)

## Aims

● To develop and understand a simple hydraulic system, which works because of air pressure.
● To consider ways in which this principle is applied to everyday life and objects around us.
● To understand how air pressure/hydraulics are used to help people.

## Equipment/tools

Syringes (5/10/20 ml), syringe tube, wood, card, glue, scissors, ruler, pencil, boxes

**Some sample 'hydraulic' ideas**

## Notes

● Examples of air pressure and its usefulness should help children to begin to understand hydraulics, e.g. tyres, bicycle pump, balloons.
● Consider things that go up and down or in and out, and decide if it is air pressure or mechanical pressure that causes it. (Why do large lorries hiss when they stop or start?)

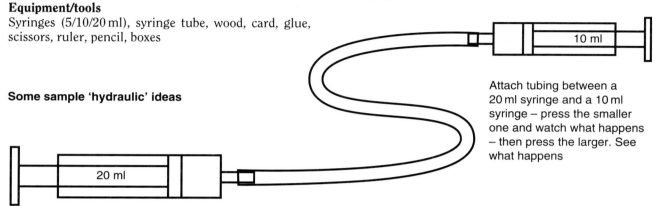

Attach tubing between a 20 ml syringe and a 10 ml syringe – press the smaller one and watch what happens – then press the larger. See what happens

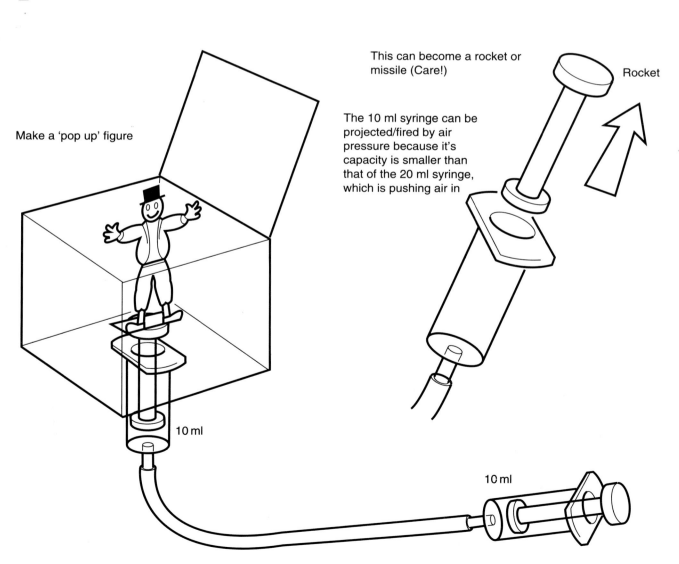

Make a 'pop up' figure

This can become a rocket or missile (Care!)

Rocket

The 10 ml syringe can be projected/fired by air pressure because it's capacity is smaller than that of the 20 ml syringe, which is pushing air in

43

# SIMPLE CIRCUIT AND SWITCH

### Aims
● To understand how a circuit works by being activated by a switch.

### Equipment/tools
Copymaster 89, battery, wire, wire strippers, crocodile clip, scissors, bulb and holder, thick card or balsa wood, paper fasteners

### For testing conductivity
Wood, plastic, foil, pencil, scouring pad, scissors, card, coal, paper, spoon

### Notes
● The task is to make a simple circuit.
● The use of wire strippers might be better done by the teacher, if considered appropriate.
● Children will have to make good connections for this to work, and it would be helpful if they could carry out conductivity tests prior to starting, or use this task as an opportunity to test for materials that will conduct electricity.
● Children could test a buzzer or motor as well as a light bulb.

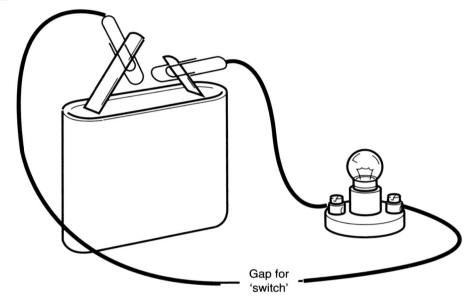

Gap for 'switch'

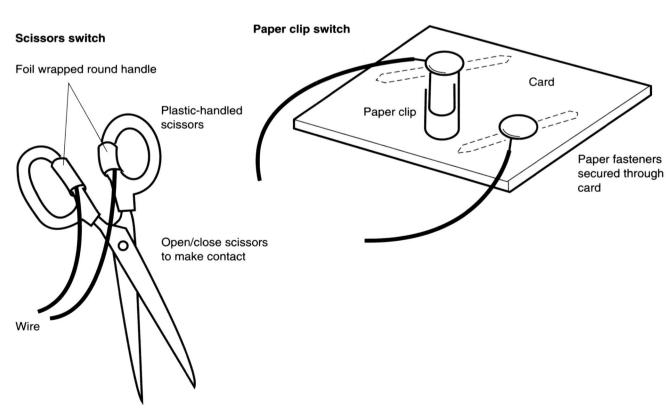

**Scissors switch**

Foil wrapped round handle

Plastic-handled scissors

Open/close scissors to make contact

Wire

**Paper clip switch**

Card

Paper clip

Paper fasteners secured through card

# CIRCUIT BOARD GAME

### Aims
● To apply knowledge of a simple circuit to a board game that involves matching words and pictures.

### Equipment/tools
Copymaster 90 (cut out the squares), cardboard, paper fasteners, wire battery, buzzers or bulb and holder, wire strippers, screwdriver

### Note
● Children can cut out the pictures and words on the Copymaster.

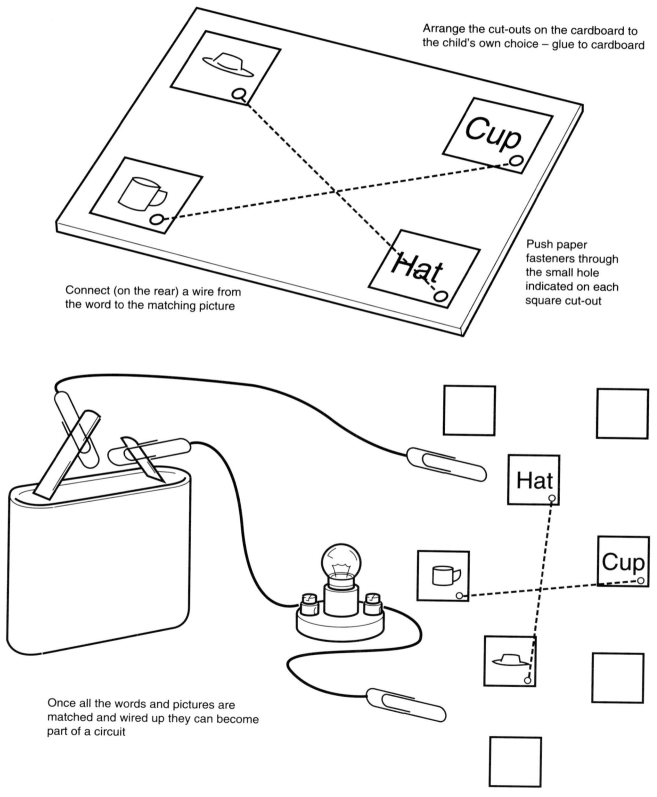

Arrange the cut-outs on the cardboard to the child's own choice – glue to cardboard

Push paper fasteners through the small hole indicated on each square cut-out

Connect (on the rear) a wire from the word to the matching picture

Once all the words and pictures are matched and wired up they can become part of a circuit

45

# PAINT SPINNER

### Aims
● To use the power of a small motor to help to make a spinning surface on which to produce an interesting pattern.

### Equipment/tools
Battery, wire, motor, card, plastic tubing, cork, paint, paper

### Note
● The children can be asked to make a circuit that includes a motor.

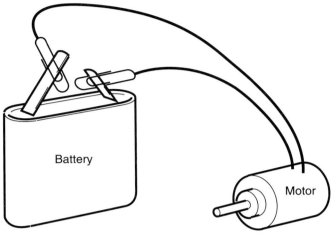

Battery

Motor

When this has been done place a cork over the motor spindle. Glue firmly a piece of card onto the surface of the cork.

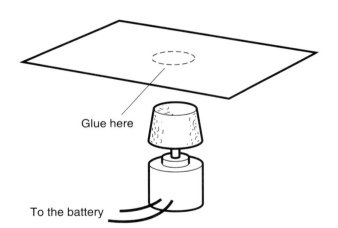

Glue here

To the battery

When the circuit is completed the card and cork should spin. Clip a piece of paper to the card (same size) and drop paint onto the paper as it spins. **Make sure the spinner is placed somewhere protected by sides to avoid splashing**

As the paint hits the paper it will splash out making some interesting patterns

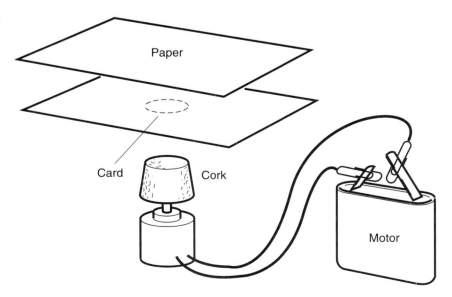

Paper

Card

Cork

Motor

# SHIPS AND BOATS ▶

## Aims
● To understand what makes a boat move in water.
● To develop awareness of what makes a ship float.
● To understand the principles of floating and sinking.

## Equipment/tools
Copymaster 92, plastic bottles, card, disks (bottle tops), elastic bands, dowel, balsa wood (for hulls), plastic tubing, garden labels, corks (plus anything considered appropriate), strong glue, nails, screws, balloons, small bottles

## Notes
● An object will float when enough water to equal its weight is displaced. (Keeping boats stable enough to float and avoid capsizing present problems that can usually be solved by 'trial and error'.)
● It is important to have material available (nails, screws, metal bars) that can be attached to the bottom of the vessel to increase stability.

**Propelled boat**

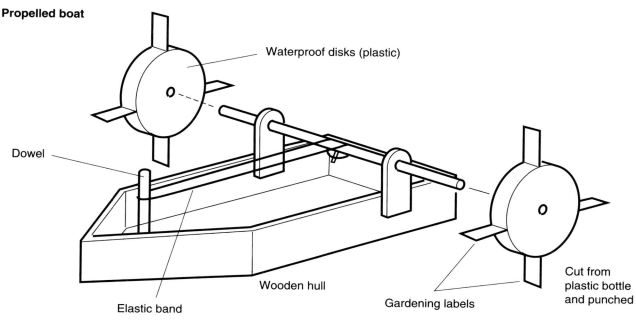

Waterproof disks (plastic)

Dowel

Elastic band

Wooden hull

Gardening labels

Cut from plastic bottle and punched

**Will the ship sink?**

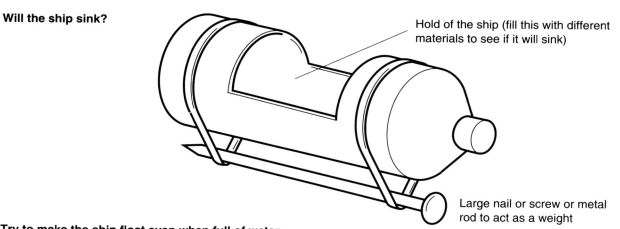

Hold of the ship (fill this with different materials to see if it will sink)

Large nail or screw or metal rod to act as a weight

**Try to make the ship float even when full of water**

Place different materials in the hold and test the ship to see if it will float or sink

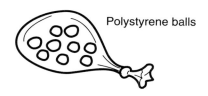

Polystyrene balls

Small plastic bottles (empty) with lid on

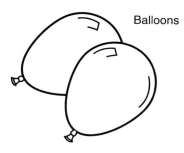

Balloons

47

# DIVING BELL

## Aims
● To understand floating and sinking principles and that an object will float when its own weight is displaced in water.

## Equipment/tools
Pen top, plastic bottle and top, Blu-tack, water

## Note
● The pen top becomes a 'diving bell' when Blu-tack is fastened around the top at the open end.

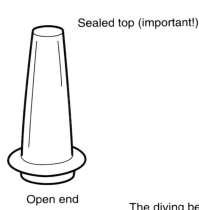

Sealed top (important!)

Open end

The diving bell is placed in a bottle full to the brim with water – take care not to spill any water – which will allow air into the bottle

Screw on the top trapping the diving bell at the top

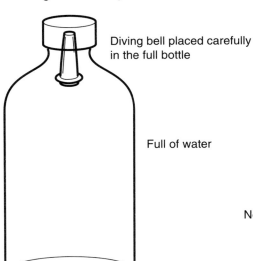

Diving bell placed carefully in the full bottle

Full of water

Next – squeeze the bottle and watch the diving bell!

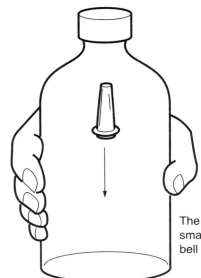

Squeeze

The diving bell has a small air bubble inside which is squashed or compressed when the bottle is squeezed

The bubble becomes smaller and the diving bell sinks

48

# PERCUSSION INSTRUMENTS

### Aims
● To appreciate that sounds can be made from simple, everyday objects, which can provide rhythm or sound effects to complement other work in the classroom.

### Equipment/tools
Copymaster 94, dowel, plastic cups and bottles, yoghurt pots, beans (dried), sandpaper, blocks of wood, sellotape, glue, washers, corks, bobbins, etc.

### Notes
● Having available a variety of containers and small items is necessary to fully explore the possibilities available when making percussion instruments, e.g. beaters, shakers, scrapers.
● This idea works well when linked to stories or poems by providing sound effects during the reading of such work.
● It may be that the children are involved with a music topic and might wish to compose musical sounds.

**Shakers**

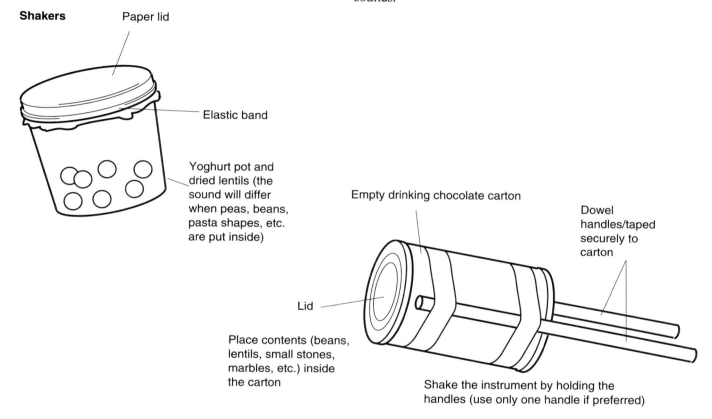

Paper lid

Elastic band

Yoghurt pot and dried lentils (the sound will differ when peas, beans, pasta shapes, etc. are put inside)

Empty drinking chocolate carton

Dowel handles/taped securely to carton

Lid

Place contents (beans, lentils, small stones, marbles, etc.) inside the carton

Shake the instrument by holding the handles (use only one handle if preferred)

**Beaters**

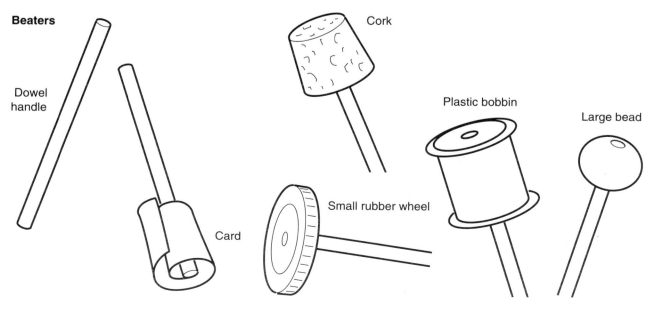

Dowel handle

Cork

Plastic bobbin

Large bead

Card

Small rubber wheel

## PERCUSSION INSTRUMENTS – continued

**Scraper**

Sandpaper glued to blocks

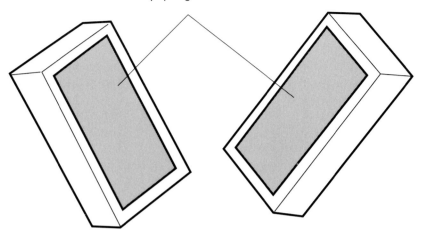

Broom handle cut

Dowel scraper

Box cut to
take blocks

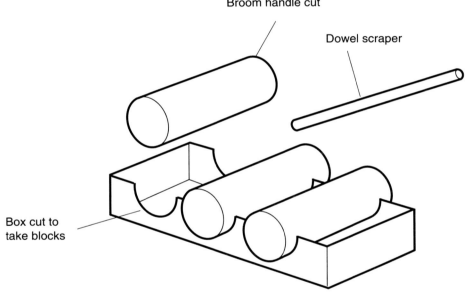

**Small blocks – held in hand**

dowel scraper

Blank matchsticks

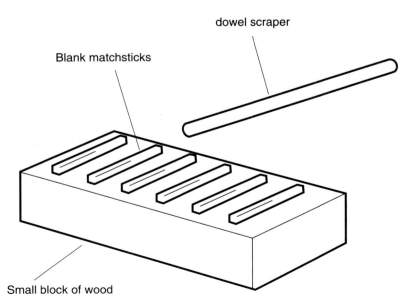

Small block of wood

50

# CREATURE WITH MOVING EARS

### Aims
● To demonstrate how a lever system can operate in conjunction with pivots (paper fasteners).

### Equipment/tools
Card, paper, colouring materials, paper fasteners, scissors, tape, glue, hole punch

### Notes
● Draw the basic head and ear shapes onto card.
● The position of the pivot holes is important and the children must consider this before punching the holes in the ears.

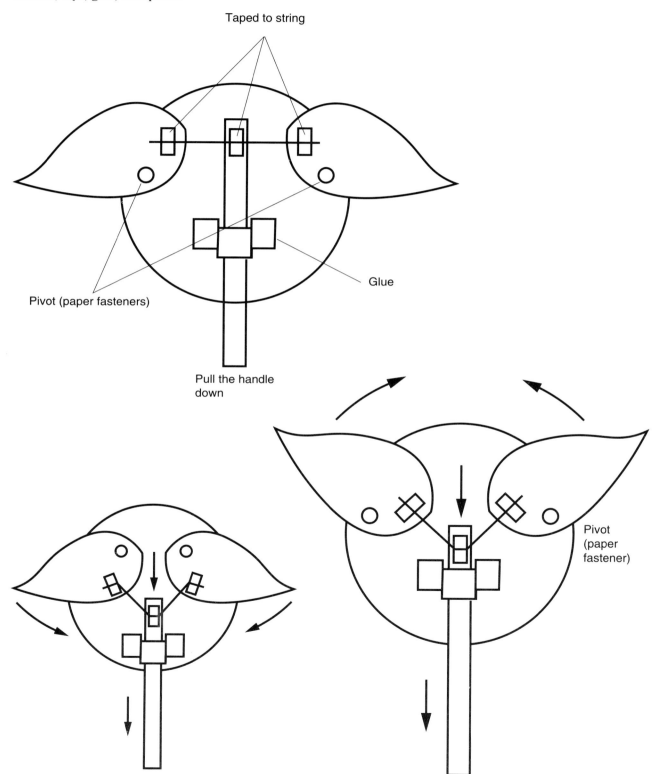

Taped to string

Pivot (paper fasteners)

Glue

Pull the handle down

Pivot (paper fastener)

51

# GATE/BARRIER

### Aims
● To demonstrate the leverage principle.
● To make a simple model barrier of the type used in car parks.

### Equipment/tools
Matchboxes, thick card, dowel, weights, hole punch, paper clips

### Notes
● The children can start to develop an understanding of the 'lowering principle'.
● The raising and lowering of objects can sometimes be made easier by implementing a leverage system to help the work-load.
● The barrier can be made to operate simply by adding or removing small weights at one end.

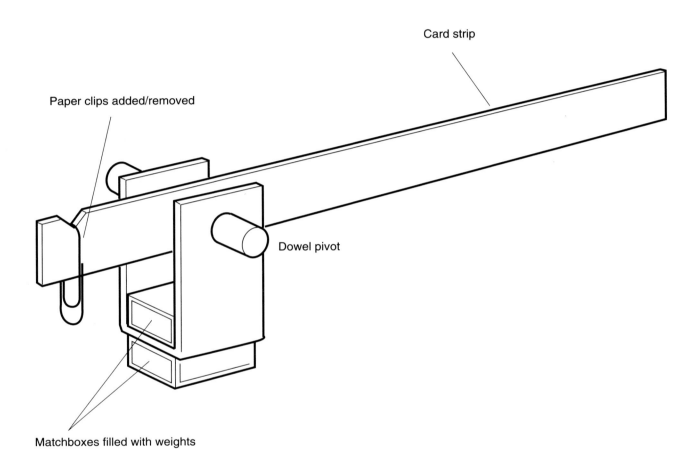

Card strip

Paper clips added/removed

Dowel pivot

Matchboxes filled with weights

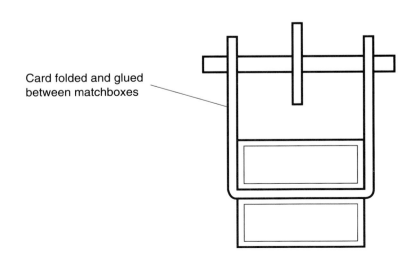

Card folded and glued between matchboxes

# BALANCING CLOWN

## Aims
● To understand that two objects will balance at a certain point, which we call the centre of gravity.
● To understand that if the weight of one of the objects changes, it will affect the centre of gravity.

## Equipment/tools
Copymaster 95, cardboard, dowel, weights, thread

## Notes
● The cut-out clown should be copied onto cardboard.
● Children can adjust or change the weight by adding Blu-tack or plasticine, or by adding small weights until the balance is achieved. The string will then be running through the centre of gravity.

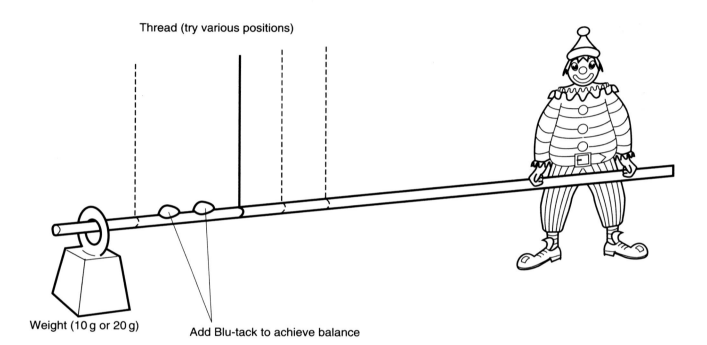

Thread (try various positions)

Weight (10 g or 20 g)

Add Blu-tack to achieve balance

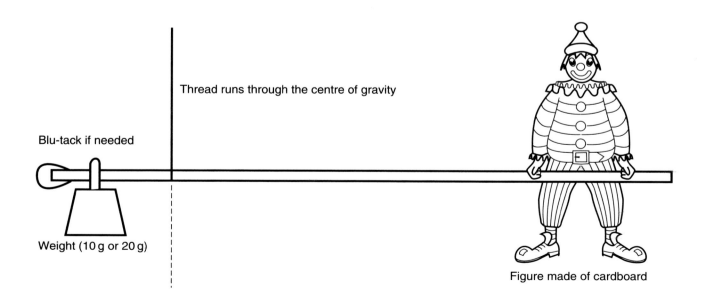

Thread runs through the centre of gravity

Blu-tack if needed

Weight (10 g or 20 g)

Figure made of cardboard

# BALANCING BIRD

### Aims
● To understand that an object will balance at a certain point called the centre of gravity.
● To understand that changes to the weight or the shape will affect the centre of gravity.

### Equipment/tools
Copymaster 96, thin modelling card, thread, Blu-tack

### Notes
● The paper shape of the bird should be copied onto card.
● The card shape is more rigid and suitable for a balancing toy.
● Blu-tack should be put onto each wing tip until balance is achieved.

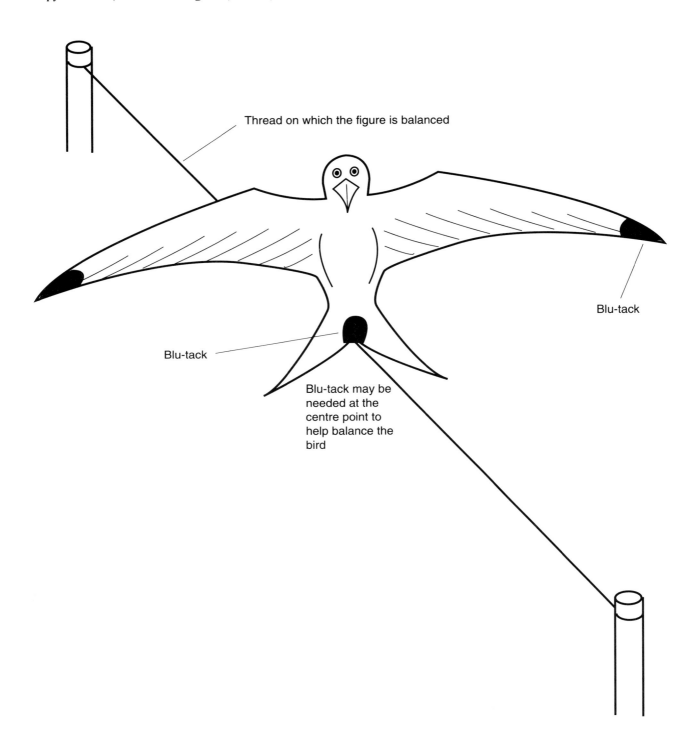

Thread on which the figure is balanced

Blu-tack

Blu-tack

Blu-tack may be needed at the centre point to help balance the bird

# CLAY WORK: 1

## Aims
● To understand that clay can be made into different shapes when it is soft, but will harden when left exposed to the air.
● To enable children to handle this material and to use 'slip' (water and clay) to help to achieve their final product.

## Note
● 'Slip' is clay and water mixed to a paste and should be applied as 'glue' when attaching small parts to the model. The children need to become accustomed to using slip, to avoid models falling apart because of the shrinkage that occurs as clay dries.

## Equipment/tools
Clay, clay board, rolling pin, clay tools, (straws, dowel and other small tools) water

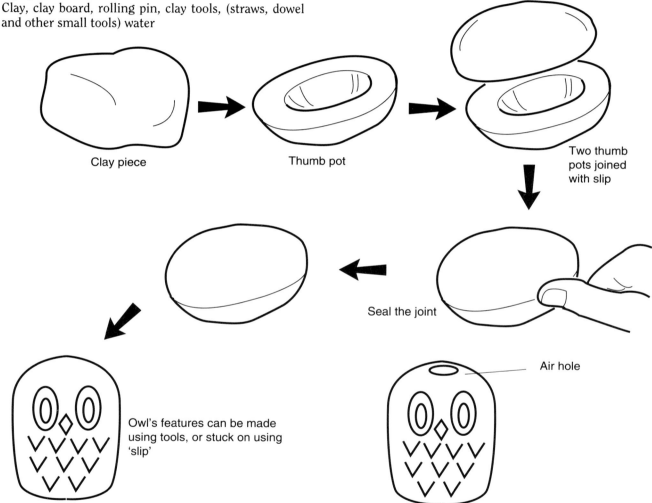

Clay piece

Thumb pot

Two thumb pots joined with slip

Seal the joint

Owl's features can be made using tools, or stuck on using 'slip'

Air hole

Caution! If you intend firing the clay in a kiln, leave a small air hole in the model or it could explode when heated!

## Other ideas

Sad face
(Happy)
(Angry)
(Puzzled)
(Scared)

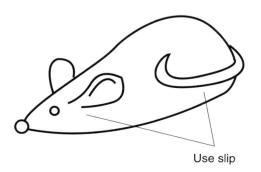

Use slip

# CLAY WORK: 2

**Aims**

● To understand the properties of clay (the difference between wet and dry).

● To produce a wall-hanging, clay 'pocket'.

**Equipment/tools**

Clay, tools, rolling pin, water

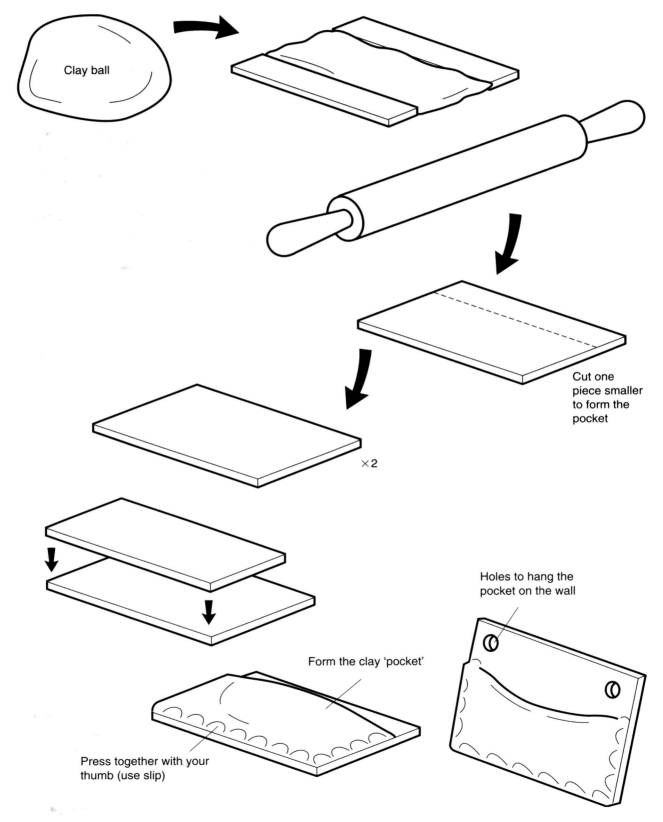

Clay ball

Cut one piece smaller to form the pocket

×2

Holes to hang the pocket on the wall

Form the clay 'pocket'

Press together with your thumb (use slip)

# POP-UP CARD

## Aims

● To work with card and paper and learn how to make a simple pop-up card.

● To develop the necessary manipulative skills involved: cutting, measuring, gluing, folding.

## Equipment/tools

Card, paper, glue, scissors, colouring materials

## Note

● The National Curriculum requires that children be given the chance to learn the characteristics and properties of a variety of materials. Paper and card are the most common, and this simple exercise will help to develop certain basic skills essential to technology.

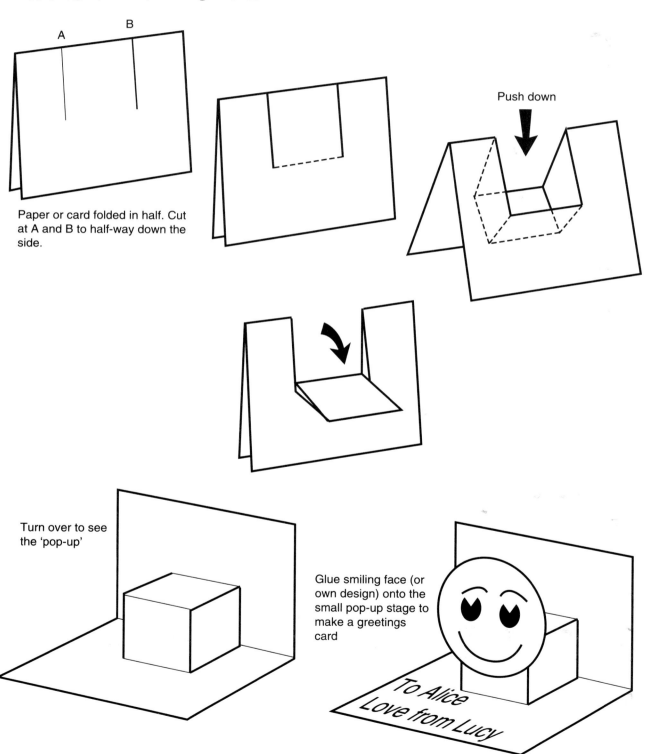

A   B

Paper or card folded in half. Cut at A and B to half-way down the side.

Push down

Turn over to see the 'pop-up'

Glue smiling face (or own design) onto the small pop-up stage to make a greetings card

To Alice
Love from Lucy

# DECORATED CARD BOX

### Aims

● To work with card to produce interesting and unusual box or lantern shapes.

### Note

● The cut-out shapes shown here are examples only.

### Equipment/tools

Thin card, scissors, glue, pencil

Draw required shape on each fold

Fold a piece of card into four
(allowing for a gluing tab)

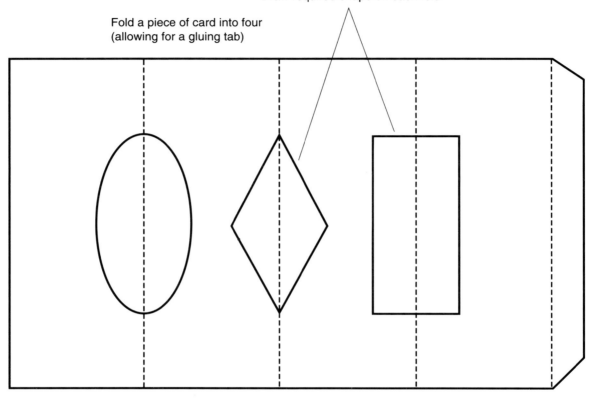

Fold the card as shown and
cut out the desired shape

Tab

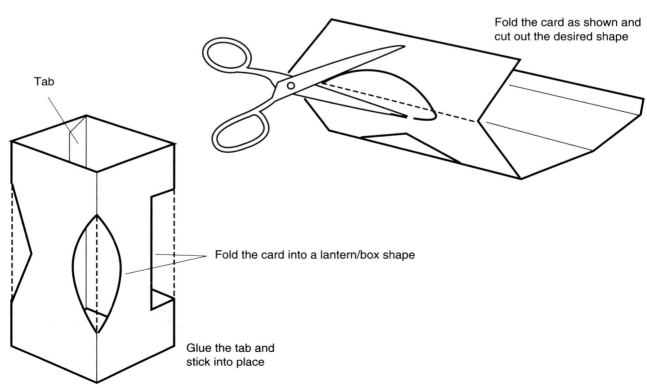

Fold the card into a lantern/box shape

Glue the tab and
stick into place

# WHERE? ▶

**Author**
**David McCord**

### Where?

Where is that little pond I wish for?
Where are those little fish to fish for?

Where is my little rod for catching?
Where are the bites that I'll be scratching?

Where is the line for which I'm looking?
Where are those handy hooks for hooking?

Where is my rusty reel for reeling?
Where is my trusty creel for creeling?

Where is the worm I'll have to dig for?
Where are the boots that I'm too big for?

Where is there *any* boat for rowing?
Where is ...
        Well, anyway, it's snowing.

*Technology ideas*
Pond
Fishing rod and reel
Fish
Worm
Boat

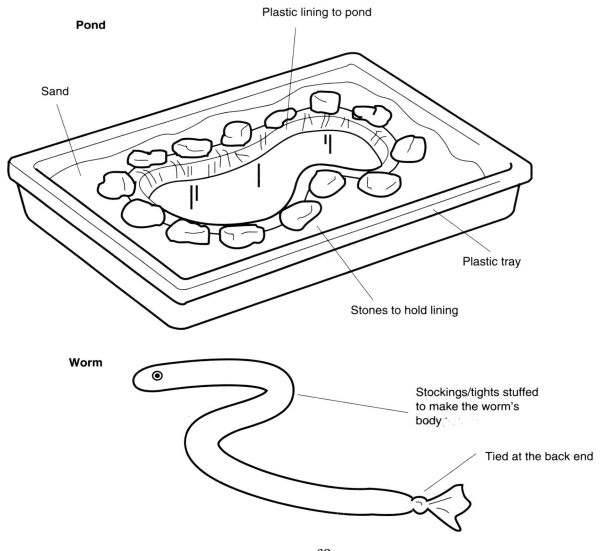

**Pond**

Plastic lining to pond

Sand

Plastic tray

Stones to hold lining

**Worm**

Stockings/tights stuffed to make the worm's body

Tied at the back end

## WHERE? – continued

**Boat**

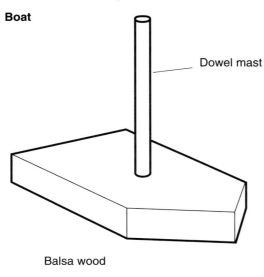

Dowel mast

Balsa wood

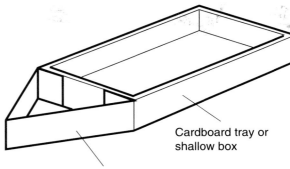

Cardboard tray or
shallow box

Card piece folded and glued to
make the pointed end of the boat

Orange peel with dowel
paddles pushed
through

**Rod and Reel**

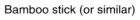
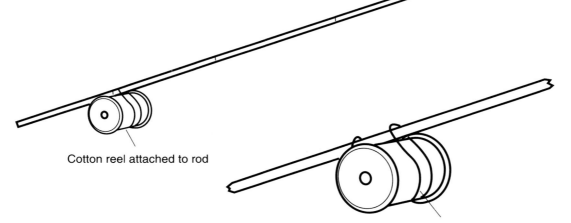

Bamboo stick (or similar)

Cotton reel attached to rod

Elastic or string wrapped round
the pole and the reel

**Fish**

Card fish decorated with patterns

Reference books could be
used to find ideas for patterns

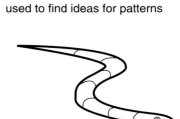

# CHRISTMAS SECRETS ▶

**Author**
**Aileen Fisher**

### Christmas Secrets

Secrets long and secrets wide,
brightly wrapped and tightly tied,

Secrets fat and secrets thin,
boxed and sealed and hidden in,

Some that rattle, some that squeak,
some that caution 'Do Not Peek' …

Hurry, Christmas, get here first,
get here fast … before we *burst*.

Children can make their own wrapped secrets and decorate them. The concept of being able to wrap a secret fires the imagination. It could be a wish, a dream, a message, a surprise, a warning or a present for someone else.

The shape and size can be left to the imagination.

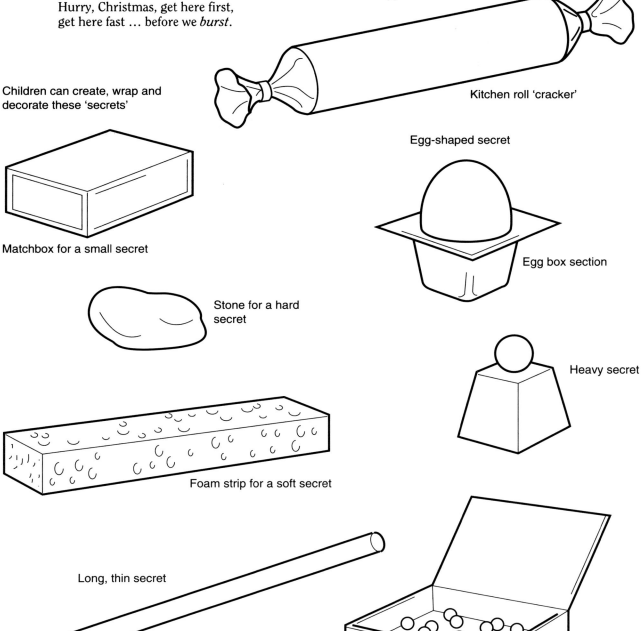

*Technology ideas*

Kitchen roll 'cracker'

Egg-shaped secret

Children can create, wrap and decorate these 'secrets'

Matchbox for a small secret

Egg box section

Stone for a hard secret

Heavy secret

Foam strip for a soft secret

Long, thin secret

Box with dried peas/beans for a secret that rattles

65

# CYCLING DOWN THE STREET TO MEET MY FRIEND JOHN

**Author**
**Gareth Owen**

### Cycling Down the Street to Meet My Friend John

On my bike and down our street,
Swinging round the bend,
Whizzing past the Library,
Going to meet my friend.

Silver flash of spinning spokes,
Whirr of oily chain,
Bump of tyre on railway line
Just before the train.

The road bends sharp at Pinfold Lane
Like a broken arm,
Brush the branches of the trees
Skirting Batty's Farm.

Tread and gasp and strain and bend
Climbing Gallows' Slope,
Flying down the other side
Like an antelope.

Swanking into Johnnie's street,
Cycling hands on hips,
Past O'Connors corner shop
That always smells of chips.

Bump the door of his back-yard
Where we always play,
Lean my bike and knock the door,
'Can John come out to play?'

This poem can be developed into technology work by introducing the idea for a street plan or map showing the route taken by the cyclist.

The various buildings and features can be placed in the correct position.

A possible street plan can be found on Copymaster 104.

# CLOCK

**Author**
**Valerie Worth**

### Clock

Clock face
This clock
has stopped,
Some gear
Or spring
Gone wrong—
Too tight,
Or cracked,
Or choked
With dust;
A year
Has passed
Since last
It said
Ting ting
Or tick
Or tock.
Poor
Clock.

*Technology ideas*

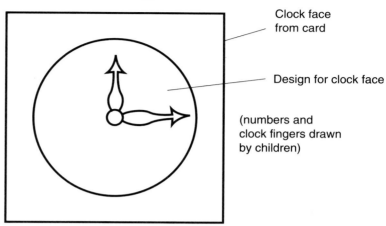

Clock face
from card

Design for clock face

(numbers and
clock fingers drawn
by children)

Characters to be
decided by children

**1,2,3,  IV,V,VI,
7,8,9,  10,11,12,**

**Cogs, Gears**

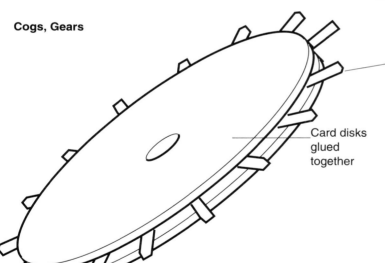

Matchsticks

Card disks
glued
together

(See 'Techniques, tools and storage'
page 86 for ideas) or use templates
(Copymaster 105)

Nuts, washers glued to
the rear of the clock face

Remember! – the clock is broken
and doesn't work!

67

# JAMAICA MARKET

**Author**
**Agnes Maxwell-Hall**

### Jamaica Market

Honey, pepper, leaf-green limes,
Pagan fruit whose names are rhymes,
Mangoes, breadfruit, ginger-roots,
Granadillas, bamboo-shoots,
Cho-cho, ackees, tangerines,
Lemons, purple Congo-beans,
Sugar, okras, kola-nuts,
Citrons, hairy coconuts,
Fish, tobacco, native hats,
Gold bananas, woven mats,
Plantains, wild-thyme, pallid leeks,
Pigeons with their scarlet beaks,
Oranges and saffron yams,
Baskets, ruby guava jams,
Turtles, goat-skins, cinnamon,
Allspice conch-shells, golden rum.
Black skins, babel – and the sun
That burns all colours into one.

*Technology ideas*
Fruits and vegetables made from clay/plasticine (coloured)

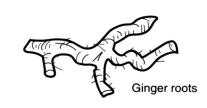

Ginger roots

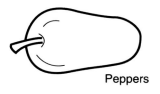

Peppers

Tangerines

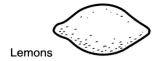

Lemons

**Hat**

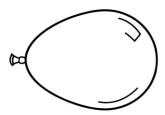

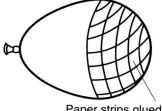

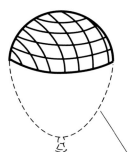

Balloon inflated to head size

Paper strips glued

Balloon removed

Straw fringe glued to base

Card headband to hold straw in place

**Shells**
It would help to have a shell collection for the children to observe while making their own from clay or plasticine

**Woven mats**

Tapestry canvas or 'Binca' material
Children can weave/embroider their design for the mat

# AT SEA IN THE HOUSE

**Author**
**Stanley Cook**

### At Sea in the House

When I pretend them to be
The tables and chairs are land
Where you can safely stand
And the carpet between is sea.

The dining table makes a boat
And I climb on there
By way of the rocking chair
And out to sea we float.

The pattern in the carpet
Swims like fish on the floor
And anyone opening the door
Is sure to get very wet.

*Technology ideas*
Table
Chair

**Table**

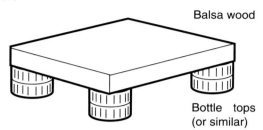

Balsa wood

Bottle tops
(or similar)

**Chair**

Empty box

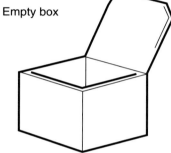

Card piece glued to
the back

Card seat folded and
glued down

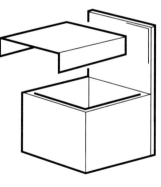

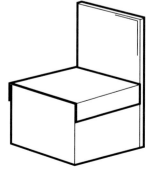

**Carpet design**
Children can use the design sheet (Copymaster 13) on
which to decide their choice of carpet pattern
(Grid Sheet – Copymaster 14)

# THE BIRD'S NEST

**Author**
**John Drinkwater**

*Technology ideas*
Bird's nest
Birds' eggs

### The Bird's Nest

I know a place, in the ivy on a tree,
Where a bird's nest is, and the eggs are three,
And the bird is brown, and the eggs are blue,
And the twigs are old, but the moss is new,
And I go quite near, though I think I should have heard
The sound of me watching, if I had been a bird.

**Bird's nest**

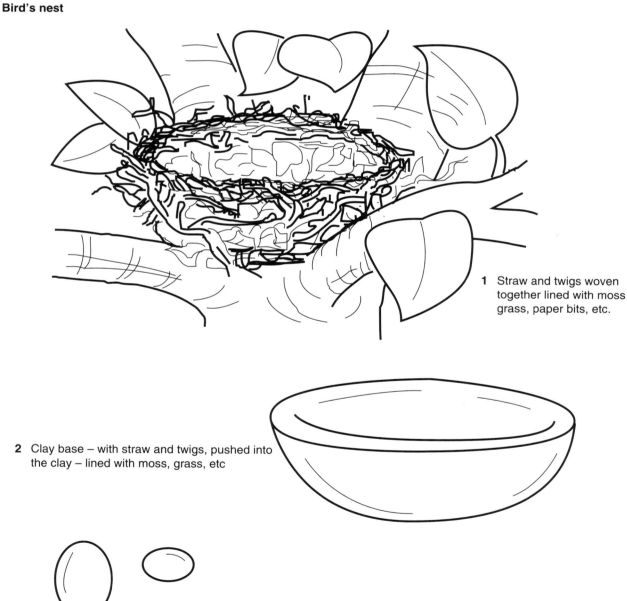

1 Straw and twigs woven together lined with moss grass, paper bits, etc.

2 Clay base – with straw and twigs, pushed into the clay – lined with moss, grass, etc

**Birds' eggs**
Made from clay and decorated (use reference books for accurate colours/patterns)

# TIGER

**Author**
**Mary Ann Hoberman**

**Technology ideas**
This poem presents an opportunity to make a tiger mask.

### Tiger

I'm a tiger
Striped with fur
Don't come near
Or I might Grrr
Don't come near
Or I might growl
Don't come near
Or I might
BITE!

Card

Draw the face of the tiger at the bottom centre of the card

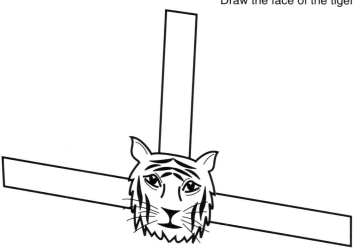

Allow for strips at the side and above the head

Bend the strips round to fit the head and glue or staple in position

Fold line

Cut a grill in the face to enable the child to see.

Don't worry about matching up the child's eyes with the tiger's eyes

Rear of mask

# TECHNOLOGY FROM STORIES

# THE TROUBLE WITH DAD ▶

**Author**
Babette Cole

**Publisher**
Heinemann

*Summary of the story*
*The Trouble with Dad* concerns a man who is bored at work. To relieve the boring life he leads, he invents a variety of robots that are designed to help other people.

Unfortunately the designs don't seem to work too well and Dad finds himself a celebrity, in demand by a television company.

Dad's inventions are very popular with others and are eventually bought from him, making Dad a wealthy man. Does this change his way of life … in some ways!

**Robots ideas
(box models)**

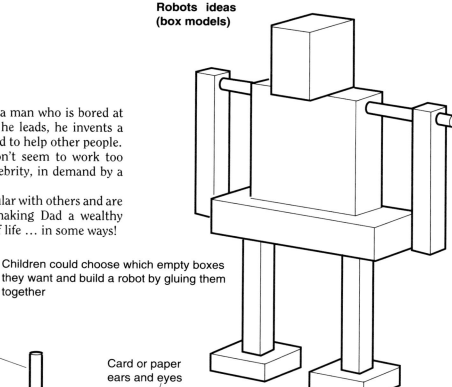

Children could choose which empty boxes they want and build a robot by gluing them together

**Robotic Grass Cutter**

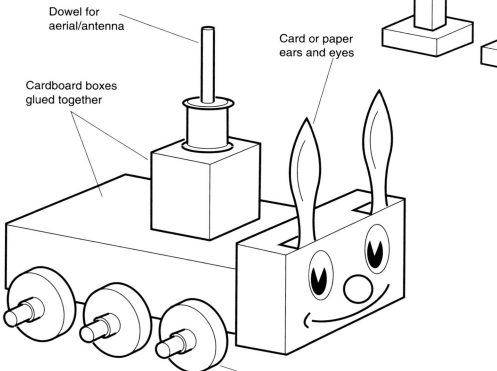

Dowel for aerial/antenna

Cardboard boxes glued together

Card or paper ears and eyes

Wheels attached to dowel axle

## THE TROUBLE WITH DAD – continued

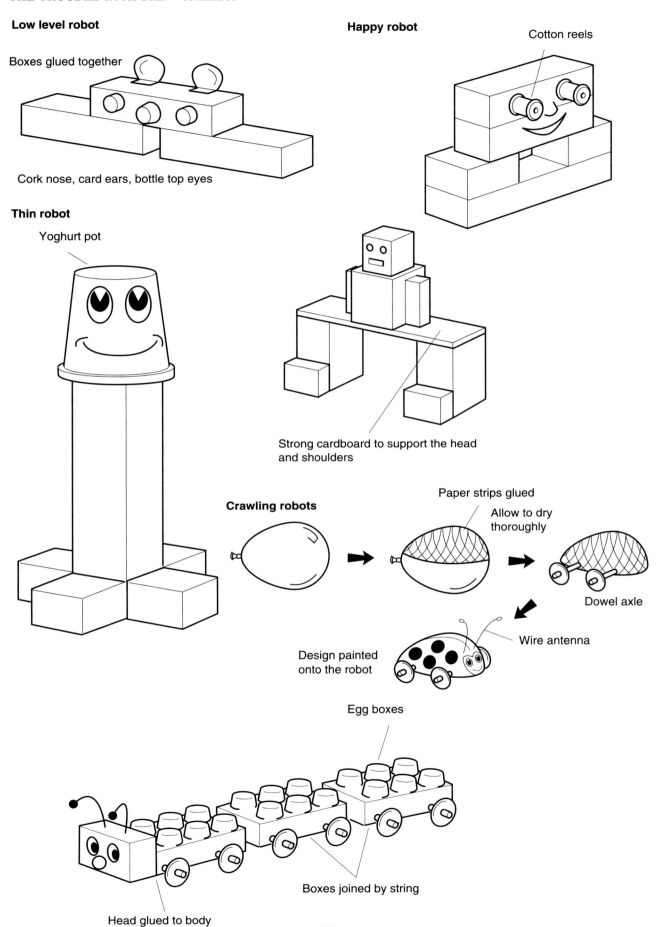

**Low level robot**

Boxes glued together

Cork nose, card ears, bottle top eyes

**Thin robot**

Yoghurt pot

**Happy robot**

Cotton reels

Strong cardboard to support the head and shoulders

**Crawling robots**

Paper strips glued

Allow to dry thoroughly

Dowel axle

Wire antenna

Design painted onto the robot

Egg boxes

Boxes joined by string

Head glued to body

73

# PINNY'S PARTY

**Author**
**Peter Firmin**

**Publisher**
**Andre Deutsch**

*Summary of the story*
Pinny and Victor are two small dolls who discover a butterfly and various children's things on the window sill. They decide to have a party, during which the butterfly wakes up. Disaster almost strikes the two dolls but they end up back in their house and boat on the shelf.

*Technology ideas*
House
Sailing boat
Dolls
Radio

**House**

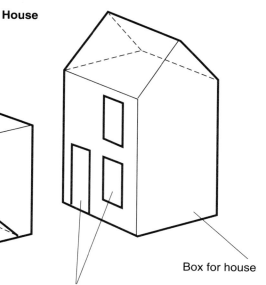

Corner of box for the roof

Box for house

Doors and windows can be stuck on or cut out

**Sailing boat**

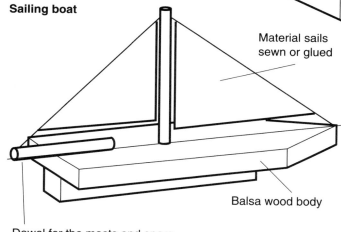

Material sails sewn or glued

Balsa wood body

Dowel for the masts and spars

**Radio**

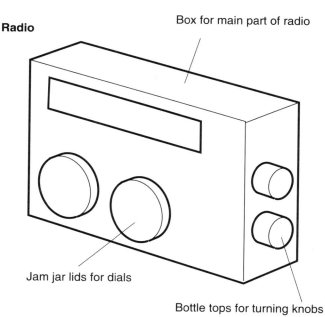

Box for main part of radio

Jam jar lids for dials

Bottle tops for turning knobs

**Dolls**

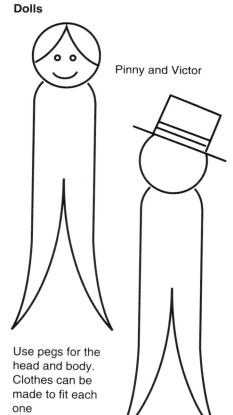

Pinny and Victor

Use pegs for the head and body. Clothes can be made to fit each one

**Butterfly**

Use Copymaster 106

74

# GRAN BUILDS A HOUSE

**Author**
**Catherine Storr**

**Publisher**
**Macdonald**

*Summary of the story*
This is a story about Gran who decides to build a doll's house. Gran uses waste material and tools to produce the house and eventually her enthusiasm leads to Grandpa helping her.

The story suggests a number of ideas for making items for the house which could easily be achieved in the classroom.

*Technology ideas*
Doll's house
Door
Wallpaper
Bath
Paintings
Frames
Mirror
People

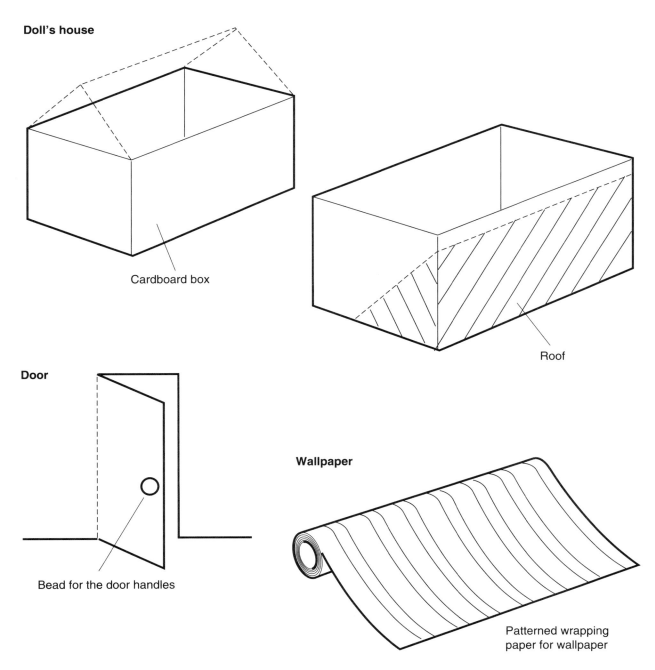

**Doll's house**

Cardboard box

Roof

**Door**

Bead for the door handles

**Wallpaper**

Patterned wrapping paper for wallpaper

## GRAN BUILDS A HOUSE – continued

**Bath**

Margarine/yoghurt pot for a bath

**Paintings**

Pictures cut from magazines as paintings for the walls

**Frames**

Card frames for pictures

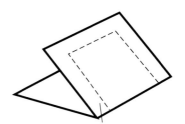

Fold into two and cut on dotted line

**Mirror**

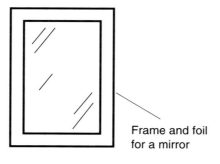

Frame and foil for a mirror

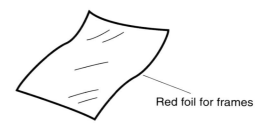

Red foil for frames

**People**

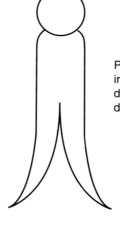

Peg people who live in the house can be dressed and decorated

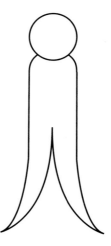

# MY PRESENTS

**Author**
**Rod Campbell**

**Publisher**
**Macmillan**

*Summary of the story*
This book tells the reader about the presents given at a birthday party. It is a 'lift the flap' book that children in school could easily re-create – with their own ideas for gifts.

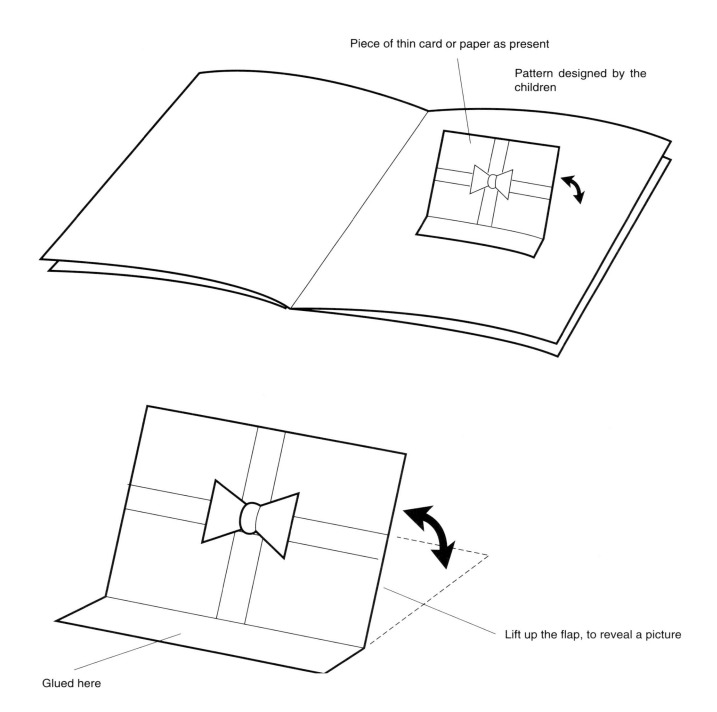

Piece of thin card or paper as present

Pattern designed by the children

Lift up the flap, to reveal a picture

Glued here

# WHAT'S THE TIME MR. WOLF

**Author**
**Colin Hawkins**

**Publisher**
**Fontana Picture Lions (Collins group)**

*Summary of the story*
The story line depicts Mr. Wolf's day, from rising in the morning to going to bed in the evening.

Mr. Wolf rises, eats breakfast, washes socks, cleans his house, eats lunch, goes shopping, plays with a ball, watches television, eats his tea, has a bath and goes to bed.

The clocks featured are all different in size, shape and the time on the clock face.

*Technology ideas*
Various sizes, shapes and different clock faces can be made by the children.

Copymasters 107–8 have blank clock faces on which the children can design their own clocks.

**Clocks**

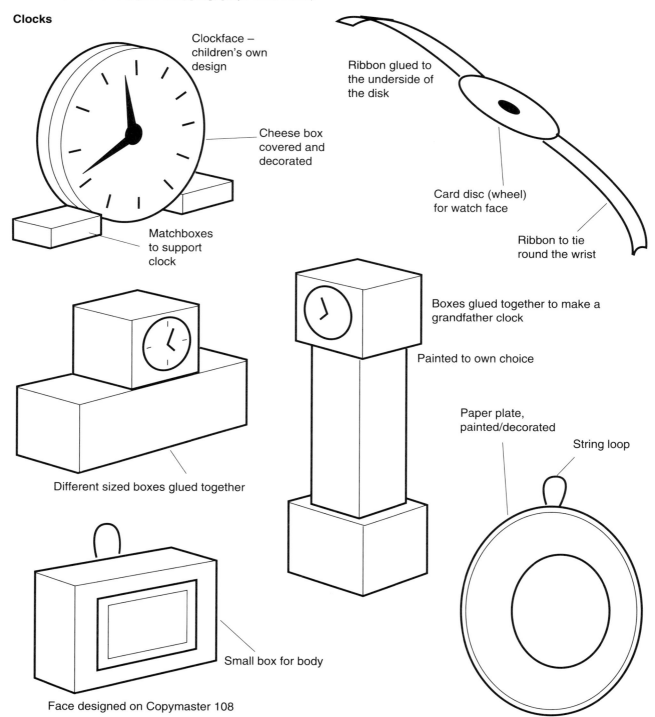

Clockface – children's own design

Cheese box covered and decorated

Matchboxes to support clock

Ribbon glued to the underside of the disk

Card disc (wheel) for watch face

Ribbon to tie round the wrist

Different sized boxes glued together

Boxes glued together to make a grandfather clock

Painted to own choice

Paper plate, painted/decorated

String loop

Small box for body

Face designed on Copymaster 108

# TECHNIQUES, TOOLS AND STORAGE

## Techniques and tools

This section gives teachers and children practical help and advice in techniques to support work in technology.

They can be used to assist work on assignments, and to develop the children's knowledge and understanding of mechanisms and structures.

Once children have become familiar with these techniques they can be applied to further projects and should assist in developing children's understanding of constructions related to technology.

## Storage

This section contains practical help for the making, in class, of storage areas as well as providing a resources checklist for the teacher.

# SIMPLE WOODEN FRAME ▶

**Simple wooden frame**

To help with a simple wooden frame construction, these cardboard triangles should be cut carefully, ensuring the triangle contains one 90° angle thus:

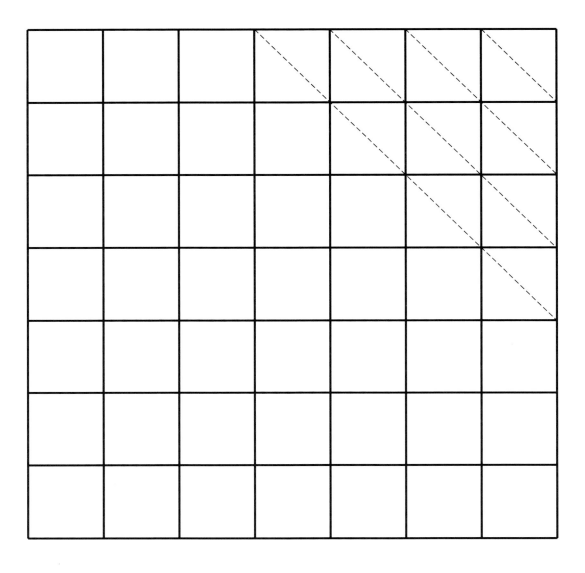

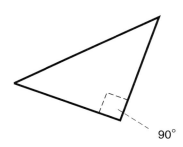

90°

The right angle will help the children's construction to be made more accurately

**WHEEL MAKING – continued**

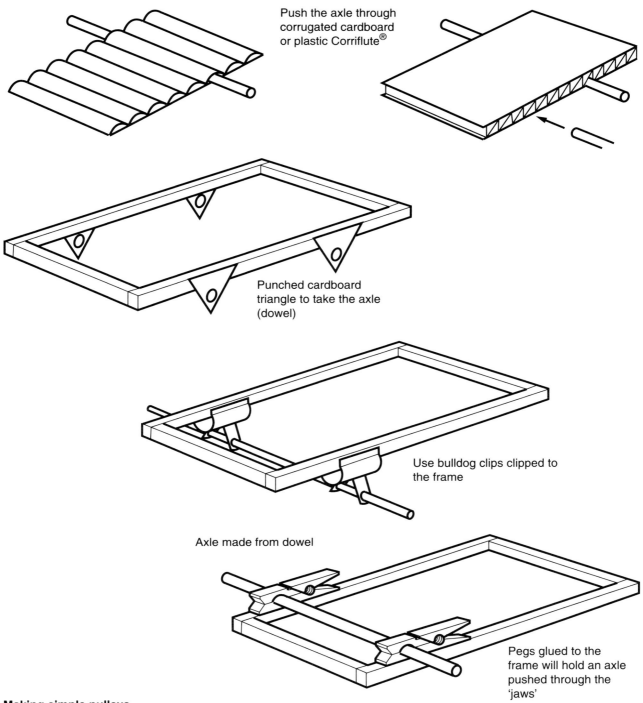

Push the axle through corrugated cardboard or plastic Corriflute®

Punched cardboard triangle to take the axle (dowel)

Use bulldog clips clipped to the frame

Axle made from dowel

Pegs glued to the frame will hold an axle pushed through the 'jaws'

**Making simple pulleys**

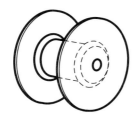

Glue two cardboard wheels to the ends of a cotton reel to make a pulley wheel

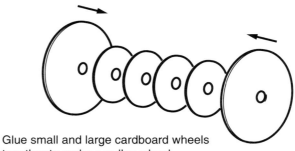

Glue small and large cardboard wheels together to make a pulley wheel

# SIMPLE MECHANISMS

## Putting pulleys to use

Free spinning bobbins (dowel axles)

A pair of 'scales' or balances using pulleys to help

500 g weight

String

500 g of marbles

Figure/shape glued to the other wheel

Elastic band tight enough to give a friction grip to both wheels

Handle

Wheel can be pulleys or bobbins

The figure will turn with the wheel

## Cog wheels

Strips of wood (lollipop type) sandwiched between two card disks

Plastic gardening labels cut to appropriate length and glued firmly to disks

Cheese box with slits cut to take strips of plastic

86

# JOINING MATERIALS

**Permanent joints**

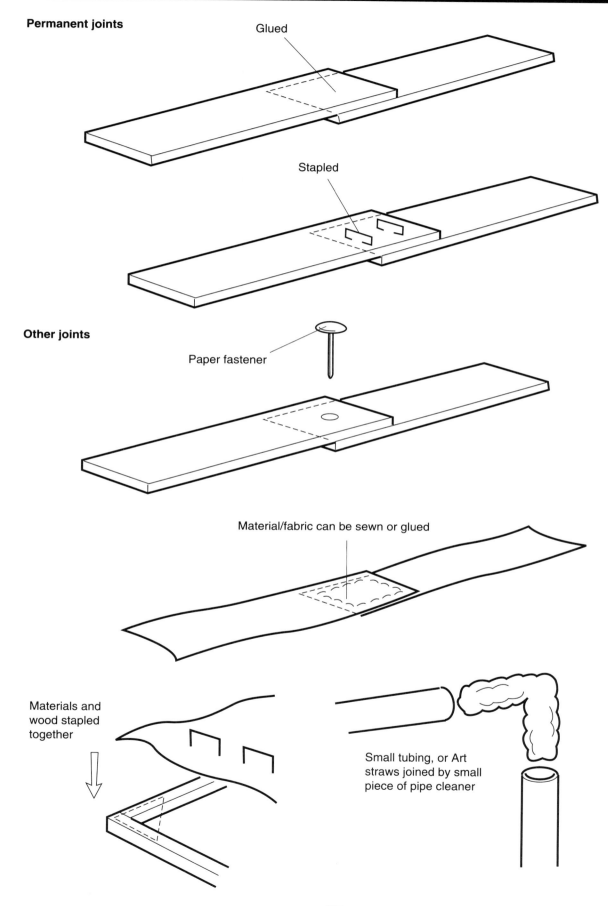

Glued

Stapled

**Other joints**

Paper fastener

Material/fabric can be sewn or glued

Materials and
wood stapled
together

Small tubing, or Art
straws joined by small
piece of pipe cleaner

## JOINING MATERIALS – continued

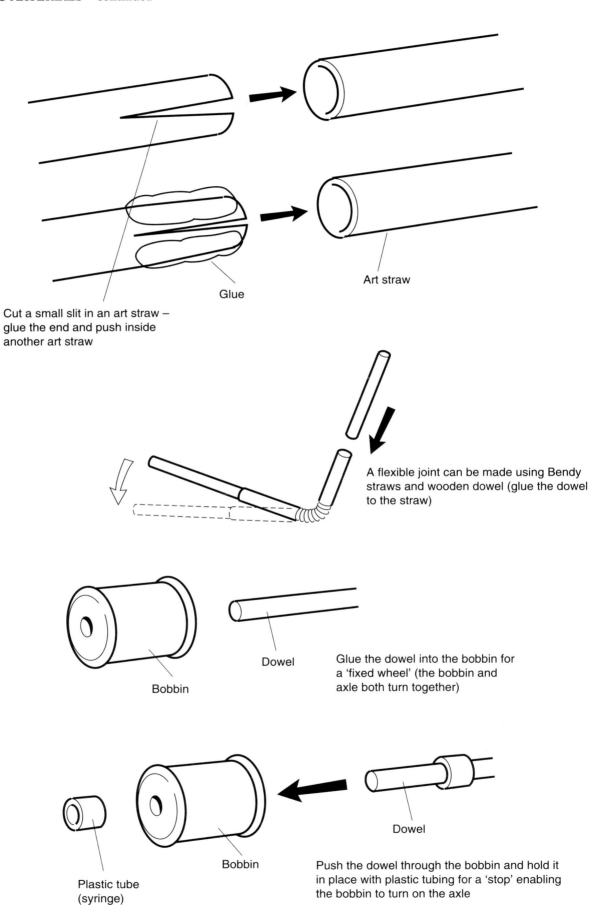

Art straw

Glue

Cut a small slit in an art straw –
glue the end and push inside
another art straw

A flexible joint can be made using Bendy
straws and wooden dowel (glue the dowel
to the straw)

Dowel

Bobbin

Glue the dowel into the bobbin for
a 'fixed wheel' (the bobbin and
axle both turn together)

Plastic tube
(syringe)

Bobbin

Dowel

Push the dowel through the bobbin and hold it
in place with plastic tubing for a 'stop' enabling
the bobbin to turn on the axle

# SIMPLE ELECTRICAL CIRCUITS

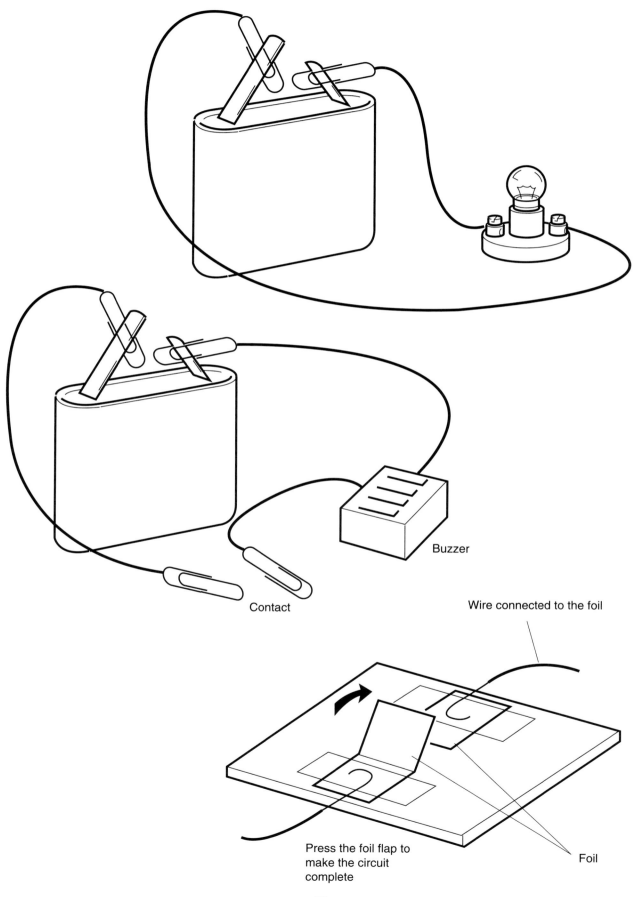

Buzzer

Contact

Wire connected to the foil

Press the foil flap to
make the circuit
complete

Foil

# USING A BENCH HOOK

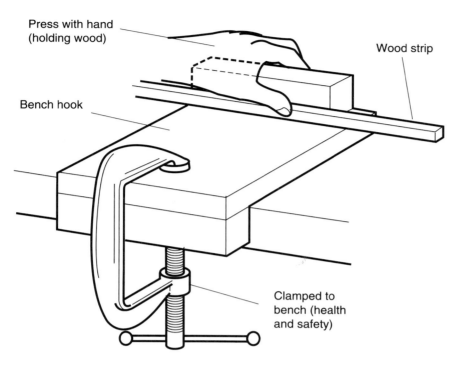

Press with hand
(holding wood)

Wood strip

Bench hook

Clamped to
bench (health
and safety)

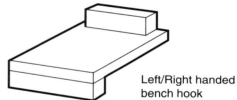

Left/Right handed
bench hook

**Measuring**

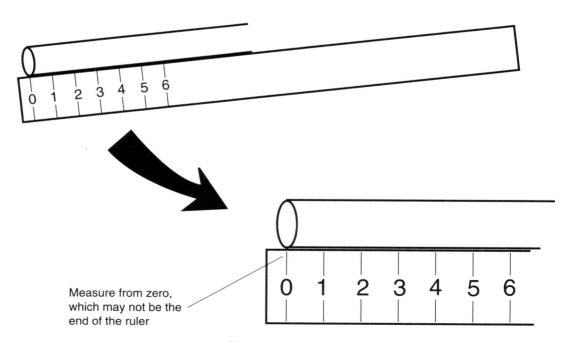

Measure from zero,
which may not be the
end of the ruler

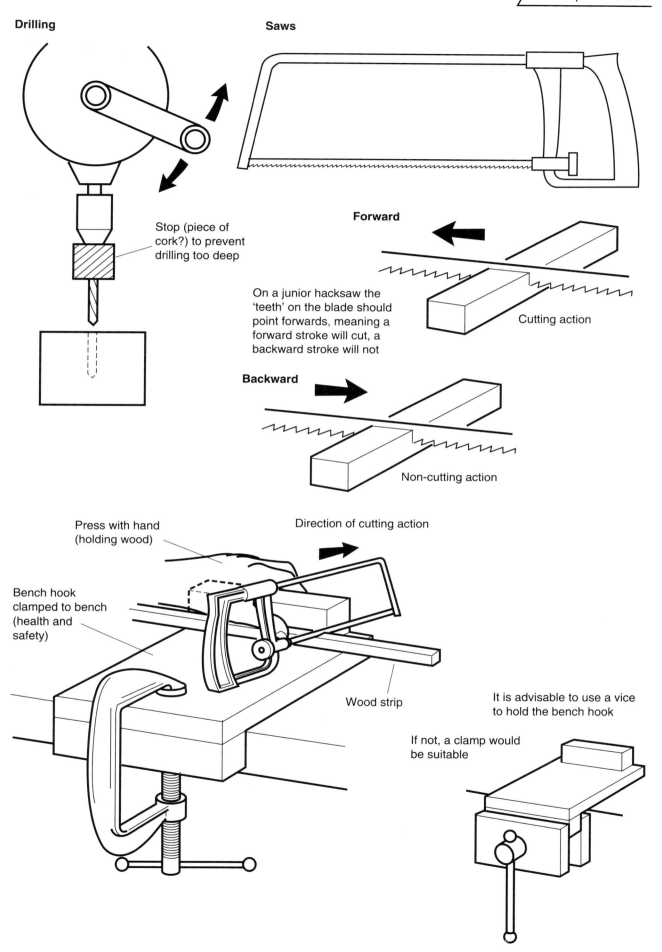

**Drilling**

**Saws**

Stop (piece of cork?) to prevent drilling too deep

**Forward**

On a junior hacksaw the 'teeth' on the blade should point forwards, meaning a forward stroke will cut, a backward stroke will not

Cutting action

**Backward**

Non-cutting action

Press with hand (holding wood)

Direction of cutting action

Bench hook clamped to bench (health and safety)

Wood strip

It is advisable to use a vice to hold the bench hook

If not, a clamp would be suitable

91

**Using scissors**

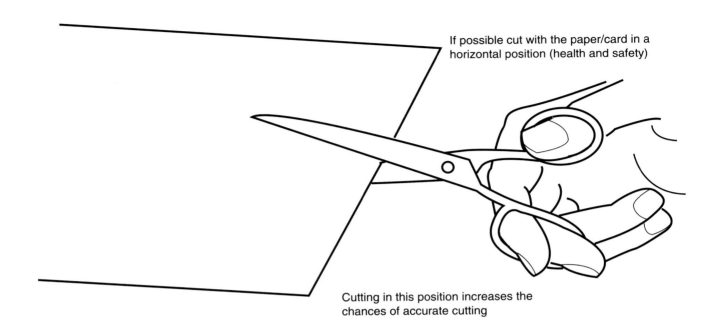

If possible cut with the paper/card in a
horizontal position (health and safety)

Cutting in this position increases the
chances of accurate cutting

When cutting zig-zags *always cut in from
the edge* of the paper

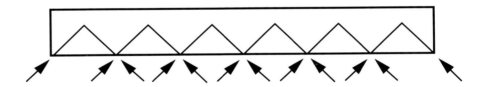

Always cut from the edge, making separate cuts

# STORAGE IDEAS

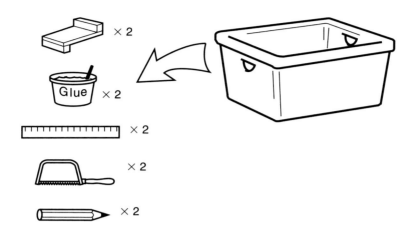

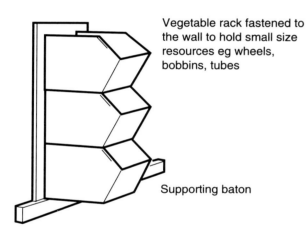

Vegetable rack fastened to the wall to hold small size resources eg wheels, bobbins, tubes

Supporting baton

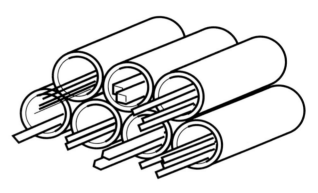

Dowel/small section wood can be stored in large tubes fastened together or contained in a box

Cylinders/tubes can be stored vertically in a box

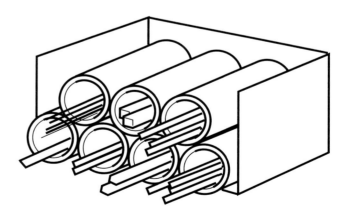

Cutlery trays can be used to store small resources ie electrical equipment, batteries, bulbs, wires, buzzers, motors

# RESOURCES CHECKLIST

**Tools**
Hacksaw and blades
Hammer
Drill and bits
Drill stand
Bench hook
Screwdriver
Scissors
Stapler and staples

**Equipment**
Pencil
Ruler
Scissors
Hole punch
Paper fasteners
String and thread
Bulldog clip
Masking tape
Sellotape®
Wood (8 mm square)
Dowel
Glue spreader
Glue
Card wheels
Wooden wheels
Corks
Marker pens
Batteries (various)

Crocodile clips
Electric wire
Bulbs
Buzzers
Motors
Paper clips
Drawing pins
Hooks and eyes
Buttons
Elastic bands
Marbles
Lollipop sticks
Matchstick blanks
Beads
Felt tip pens
Modelling wire

**Other materials**
Plastic bottles (various sizes)
Egg boxes
Bendy straws
Foil
Boxes and cartons
Pipe lagging
Foam
Material pieces
(Felt, wool)
Scrap card and paper

# RECORD-KEEPING SHEETS

**Technology National Curriculum Record**

*Attainment Target 1: Designing*

| Level | Designing | |
|-------|-----------|---|
| 1 | Generate ideas through shaping assembling and rearranging materials and components. Recognise the simple features of familiar products and where prompted relate them to their own ideas. Use pictures and words to convey what they want to do. | ☐ ☐ ☐ |
| 2 | Use their experience of materials techniques and products to help generate ideas. Use models and pictures to develop and communicate their designs. Reflect on their ideas and suggest improvements. | ☐ ☐ ☐ |
| 3 | Recognise that their designs will have to satisfy conflicting requirements. Make realistic suggestions about how they can achieve their intentions and suggest more ideas when asked. Draw on their knowledge and understanding to help them generate ideas. Use labelled sketches to show the details of their designs. | ☐ ☐ ☐ |

Key

◹ Introduced

☒ Experienced

▨ Understood/Achieved

**Technology National Curriculum Record**

*Attainment Target 2: Making*

| Level | Making | |
|-------|--------|---|
| 1 | Explain what they are making and which materials they are using.<br>Select from a narrow range of materials and use techniques and tools to shape, assemble and join them. | ☐☐☐ |
| 2 | Select from a range of materials, tools and techniques explaining their choice.<br>Manipulate tools safely and assemble and join materials in a variety of ways.<br>Make judgements about the outcome of their work. | ☐☐☐ |
| 3 | Think ahead about the order of their work choosing tools, materials and techniques more purposefully.<br>Use tools with some accuracy and use simple finishing techniques to improve their products.<br>Cut and shape materials with some precision to help assembly.<br>Their product is similar to original intentions and any changes identified. | ☐☐☐ |

Key

☑ Introduced

☒ Experienced

▩ Understood/Achieved